AMERICAN HISTORY

Early Native North Americans

Don Nardo

LUCENT BOOKS
A part of Gale, Cengage Learning

GALE
CENGAGE Learning

Detroit • New York • San Francisco • New Haven, Conn • Waterville, Maine • London

© 2008 Gale, Cengage Learning

LIBRARY OF CONGRESS CATALOGING-IN-PUBLICATION DATA

Nardo, Don, 1947–
  Early Native North Americans / by Don Nardo.
    p. cm. — (American history)
  Includes bibliographical references and index.
  ISBN 978-1-4205-0034-9 (hardcover)
  1. Indians of North America—History—Juvenile literature. 2. Paleo-Indians—Juvenile literature. 3. United States—History—Juvenile literature. I. Title.
  E77.4.N35 2008
  970.004'97—dc22
                                                          2008009253

Lucent Books
27500 Drake Rd
Farmington Hills, MI 48331

ISBN-13: 978-1-4205-0034-9
ISBN-10: 1-4205-0034-1

Printed in the United States of America
2 3 4 5 6 7 12 11 10 09 08

Contents

Foreword

The United States has existed as a nation for just over 200 years. By comparison, Rome existed as a nation-state for more than 1000 years. Out of a few struggling British colonies, the United States developed relatively quickly into a world power whose policy decisions and culture have great influence on the world stage. What events and aspirations drove this young American nation to such great heights in such a short period of time? The answer lies in a close study of its varied and unique history. As James Baldwin once remarked, "American history is longer, larger, more various, more beautiful, and more terrible than anything anyone has ever said about it."

The basic facts of United States history—names, dates, places, battles, treaties, speeches, and acts of Congress—fill countless textbooks. These facts, though essential to a thorough understanding of world events, are rarely compelling for students. More compelling are the stories in history, the experience of history.

Titles in this series explore the history of the country and the experiences of Americans. What influences led the colonists to risk everything and break from Britain? Who was the driving force behind the Constitution? Which factors led thousands of people to leave their homelands and settle in the United States? Questions like these do not have simple answers; by discussing them, however, we can view the past as a more real, interesting, and accessible place.

Students will find excellent tools for research and investigation in every title. Lucent Books' American History series provides not only facts, but also the analysis and context necessary for insightful critical thinking about history and about current events. Fully cited quotations from historical figures, eyewitnesses, letters, speeches, and writings bring vibrancy and authority to the text. Annotated bibliographies allow students to evaluate and locate sources for further investigation. Sidebars highlight important and interesting figures, events, or related primary source excerpts. Timelines, maps, and full color images add another dimension of accessibility to the stories being told.

It has been said the past has a history of repeating itself, for good and ill. In these pages, students will learn a bit about both and, perhaps, better understand their own place in this world.

ca. 77,000–75,000
As sea levels drop, the Bering Ice Bridge forms, creating a strip of land between Siberia and Alaska.

753
Traditional date for the founding of Rome, in western Italy.

ca. 500
A prince who will later become the Buddha, or "Enlightened One," is born in northern India.

ca. 8,000
The date established by scholars for the end of the Paleo-Indian phase and start of the Archaic Indian period.

ca. 3300–3000
The Sumerians build the world's first cities near the Persian Gulf, in Mesopotamia.

44
The renowned Roman military general and politician Julius Caesar is assassinated.

B.C.	75,000	12,000	8000	3000	1000	500	100

ca. 12,000
Approximate date that Siberian hunter-gatherers begin migrating across the land bridge into North America.

ca. 2200–1400
The Minoans create a sophisticated civilization, including giant palace-centers, on the large Greek island of Crete.

ca. 300
The mound-building Hopewell Indian culture begins spreading its influence through what is now the eastern United States.

ca. 1000
The mound-building Adena Indian culture begins to thrive in the Ohio River valley.

ca. 100
Indian groups living in the eastern Great Plains begin practicing agriculture.

the Early Native North Americans

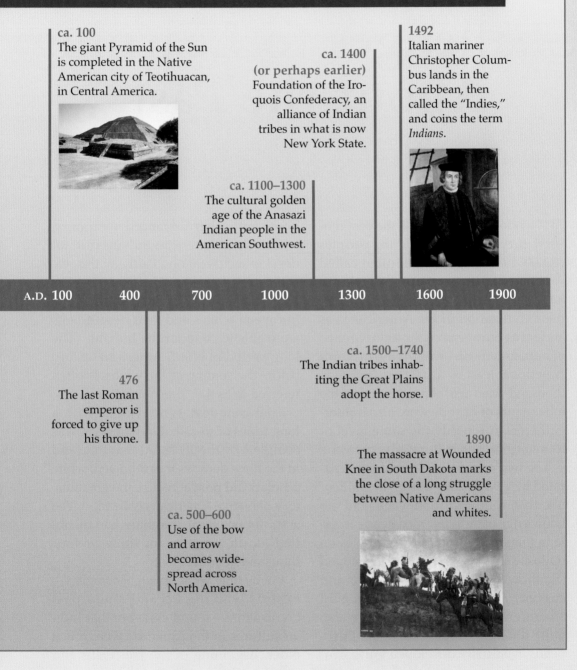

ca. 100
The giant Pyramid of the Sun is completed in the Native American city of Teotihuacan, in Central America.

ca. 1400 (or perhaps earlier)
Foundation of the Iroquois Confederacy, an alliance of Indian tribes in what is now New York State.

1492
Italian mariner Christopher Columbus lands in the Caribbean, then called the "Indies," and coins the term *Indians*.

ca. 1100–1300
The cultural golden age of the Anasazi Indian people in the American Southwest.

A.D. 100   400   700   1000   1300   1600   1900

476
The last Roman emperor is forced to give up his throne.

ca. 1500–1740
The Indian tribes inhabiting the Great Plains adopt the horse.

1890
The massacre at Wounded Knee in South Dakota marks the close of a long struggle between Native Americans and whites.

ca. 500–600
Use of the bow and arrow becomes widespread across North America.

Introduction

Challenges to Learning About the Past

Evidence unearthed in the past century has shown that the peoples who today are most often called American Indians, or Native Americans, have an extremely long history. In fact, their civilization in the Americas is as ancient as European civilization. Groups of hunter-gatherers were living in North America at least by 12,000 B.C. (fourteen thousand years ago). And at that time the inhabitants of Europe were also hunter-gatherers at roughly the same level of technological and cultural advancement.

The two civilizations remained separated by a vast ocean during the millennia that followed, and each had no knowledge of the other's existence. In the long march of centuries, the peoples on opposite sides of the Atlantic developed significantly different cultural ideas and customs. And the levels of technological advancement they achieved were also quite different. In particular, the Europeans eventually developed guns, cannons, and other advanced weaponry, whereas the American Indians did not develop such weapons. Partly for this reason, after contact between the two civilizations occurred in the late 1400s, the European whites and their descendants were able to conquer the Indians. (The long period of North American history before the coming of the whites is often referred to as the "precontact" era.)

That conquest, synonymous with a long series of so-called Indian wars, was complete by the 1890s. At that time and in the three decades that followed, white scholars did not yet realize the great history of Native American civilization. The assumption was that Indians had inhabited North America for three or four thousand years at most.

But as time went on, archaeologists—experts who dig up and study past civilizations—found evidence that Indian cultures in the Americas were much older. Beginning in the late 1940s and early 1950s, there occurred a sort of rebirth of excavations and discoveries relating to precontact Indian civilization. And today numerous digs continue at sites across the continent. These explorations provide valuable evidence for how early American Indians migrated, hunted, grew crops, traded, and waged war.

A Culture Gap

However, the work of unearthing the secrets of the ancient Native Americans is sometimes hampered by what is best described as a "culture gap" between archaeologists and Indians. True, some tribes have their own archaeologists. The Zunis and Hopis in the southwestern United States, for example, conduct digs and studies related to their own histories. (The Zunis have developed the Zuni Archaeological Program, or ZAP.) And the Mashantucket Pequots in Connecticut have operated an extensive archaeological program on their reservation since 1983. Among other discoveries, they found a nine-thousand-year-old hunting camp and a fort dating to 1675. Thousands of artifacts unearthed by the excavators can be seen in the tribe's state-of-the-art museum, which opened in 1998.

These tribal excavations are the exception rather than the rule, though. Most archaeologists who dig up past Indian cultures are white. And many Native Americans view their excavations with some degree of suspicion and/or discomfort. This stems mainly from a difference in the way Indians and whites view digging up the graves and handling the remains of buried ancestors. Most white archaeologists believe that such excavations are justified because they advance human knowledge. In contrast, many Indians see tampering with burial sites as a serious spiritual violation. "The field of archaeology is a discipline that has been little understood in the Native American community," Zuni scholar Edmund J. Ladd points out.

Digging about in the ancient tombs and robbing graves are activities Native Americans associate with witchcraft and consider to be fraught with the danger of [spiritual] contamination and death. Traditionally,

The Mashantucket Pequot Museum in Connecticut is the world's largest Native American museum. Many scholars of Indian civilization are white, which offends some Native Americans.

most Indian people would not consider digging up another human being's remains.[1]

Native American scholars like Ladd say that another aspect of the culture gap between Indian traditionalists and modern archaeologists is the way Indians have long viewed their own past. Whites have tended to have a strong fascination for what their own distant ancestors did. Many Indians, by contrast, have been more oriented toward their present and future and fairly uninterested in their dim past. "Why dwell on the past?" one Native American elder said. "We have already been there . . . and we can't do anything to change it."[2]

Efforts to Rebury Human Remains

During most of the twentieth century, numerous American Indian communities regretted the excavation of ancient burials so much that they lobbied Congress to protect the gravesites. This effort reached its highest point in the 1990 Native American Grave Protection and

Museums Must Return Native American Artifacts Under NAGPRA, as of 11-30-2006	
Human remains:	31,995 individuals
Associated funerary objects:	669,554 (includes many small items, such as beads)
Unassociated funerary objects:	118,227 (includes many small items, such as beads)
Sacred objects:	3,584
Objects of cultural patrimony:	281
Objects that are both sacred and patrimonial:	764

Taken from: National NAGPRA, National Park Service, U.S. Department of the Interior. Available online at: http://www.nps.gov/history/nagpra/.

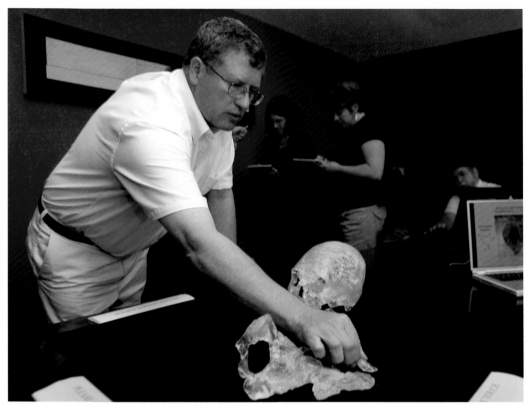

Archeologist Doug Owsley arranges the pieces of a model of Kennewick Man at the Smithsonian Museum in Washington, DC. The ownership of the actual remains of Kennewick Man is in dispute.

Repatriation Act (NAGPRA). This law requires that all Indian remains and cultural objects found on tribal or federal lands be turned over to the appropriate tribal authorities. Said officials will then rebury these artifacts, which cannot be dug up later. Also, certain kinds of Native American remains housed in museums and private collections can be reclaimed and buried by tribal authorities.

The effects of NAGPRA on North American archaeology may turn out to be significant. Hundreds of thousands of fragments of American Indian remains presently exist in public and private collections. Archaeologists worry, scholar Brian M. Fagan says,

> that much of their scientific database for studying such topics as ancient diseases and diet will be lost forever with systematic reburial of ancient populations. They argue that reburial would deprive future generations of vital scientific information. Others, including many archaeologists, believe that reburial [is an] ethical issue and should outweigh any scientific gain.[3]

Legal clashes have already occurred between supporters of NAGPRA and archaeologists who feel restricted by it. Perhaps the best known case is that of Kennewick Man. This is the name given to an ancient set of human remains found in the Columbia River in Washington State in 1996. Anthropologist James Chatters and other experts examined the remains. They think that Kennewick Man is six to nine thousand years old and that he may not belong to the same central Asian racial group that gave rise to most other ancient Native Americans. Further studies may reveal whether he was Caucasian (white), as Chatters suspects he may have been. (If Kennewick Man *was* Caucasian, the question will become: How did he get to North America thousands of years before Columbus?) Meanwhile, a local Washington tribe, the Umatilla, has claimed the remains under the provisions of NAGPRA. Tribal officials say they want to bury Kennewick Man in a secret location. At the moment, the dispute is still in the courts. So for the time being the controversial bones are housed for safe keeping in the Burke Museum of Natural History and Culture in Seattle.

The outcome of the case will likely have a bearing on future cooperation, or lack thereof, between archaeologists and various tribes. It may end up being only one of many challenges to learning about North America's distant past. But Fagan, among others, is optimistic that the disagreements that led to the creation of NAGPRA will give way "to a new era in which both groups cooperate, [although] somewhat cautiously." If a spirit of trust can be achieved, he says, "the results can be rewarding." Indeed, discovering the details of when and how American Indians populated the continent can only be accomplished conclusively through archaeological excavation. And "the future of North American archaeology," Fagan points out, "lies in collaborative research, in which Native Americans play a leading role."[4]

Chapter One

Origins of the American Indians

The most familiar history of the North American Indians is the one that begins with their "discovery" by Christopher Columbus in 1492. An Italian explorer sponsored by the Spanish crown, Columbus sailed westward across the Atlantic, hoping to reach the "Indies," a term then used to describe the coasts and islands of eastern Asia. As everyone now knows, Columbus and his men never reached Asia. Instead, they stumbled on a large land mass previously unknown to European civilization.

This new continent (now divided into two continents—North and South America) was inhabited by people very different from any whom Europeans had ever encountered. Thinking he was in the Indies, Columbus gave them the name Indians. And although it was and remains a misnomer, it is still the most common term for them, though the more recent term Native Americans is used almost as often. Columbus described these natives in his log:

> They seemed on the whole to me, to be a very poor people. They all go completely naked, even the women, though I saw but one girl. All whom I saw were young, not above thirty years of age, well made, with fine shapes and faces; their hair short, and coarse like that of a horse's tail, combed toward the forehead, except a small portion which they suffer to hang down behind, and never cut. Some paint themselves with black . . . others with white, others with red, and others with such colors as they can find. Some paint the face, and some the whole body; others only the eyes, and others the nose.[5]

Who were these people Columbus had encountered, European leaders and

Cuban natives greet Christopher Columbus and his landing party. The initial meeting between Native Americans and westerners would set the stage for misunderstanding.

scholars wondered? It was clear that the so-called Indians had a history of their own before their initial contact with white Europeans. But how long was that history? A few centuries? A few millennia? Even longer? More important, how had they come to live in the remote Americas in the first place? These questions haunted European thinkers, writers, and other observers for many generations. And numerous theories were advanced to explain the origins of the

Indians before the scholarly community firmly embraced the correct one only a few decades ago.

Native Creation Stories

The first efforts to establish how the Indians had arrived in the Americas consisted of questioning the natives directly. Once communications had been established, white leaders and missionaries asked, "Where did your people come from?" or words to that effect. The Indians had no formal histories, either written or oral, to help them answer such questions with certainty.

But the natives did have religious traditions and creation myths that had been passed down orally over many generations. Based on these stories, many Indians assumed that their tribes had always been there, at least since the Creator (often called the Great Spirit or Great Chief) had made them. Such creation tales varied from tribe to tribe and region to region; but many held similarities to that of the Chelan people of Washington State. Long ago, the story goes, the Great Chief fashioned the world.

[Then] he made the animals and the birds and gave them their names—Coyote, Grizzly Bear, Deer, Fox, Eagle, the four Wolf Brothers, Magpie, Bluejay, Hummingbird, and all the others. When he had finished his work, the creator called the animal people to him. "I am going to leave you," he said. "But I will come back. When I come again, I will make human beings. They will be in charge of you."[6]

Later, following the instructions of the Great Chief, one of the Wolf Brothers cut a beaver into twelve parts and each part grew into a different Indian tribe.

Many other Indian legends also described a great migration that had occurred in the dim past. But they were

Columbus Describes the Natives

These words are part of Christopher Columbus's initial description of the people he called Indians, entered in his log in the fall of 1492:

As I saw that they were very friendly to us, and perceived that they could be much more easily converted to our holy faith by gentle means than by force, I presented them with some red caps, and strings of beads to wear upon the neck, and many other trifles of small value, wherewith they were much delighted, and became wonderfully attached to us. Afterwards they came swimming to the boats, bringing parrots, balls of cotton thread, javelins, and many other things which they exchanged for articles we gave them, such as glass beads, and hawk's bells. . . . Weapons they have none, nor are acquainted with them, for I showed them swords which they grasped by the blades, and cut themselves through ignorance.

Internet Medieval Sourcebook, "Extracts from the Journal of Christopher Columbus." www.fordham.edu/halsall/source/columbus1.html.

not clear about where said migration had begun. Some Indians in eastern North America claimed that their ancestors had come from the "land of the setting sun," or the west; while some western Indians said the migrations began somewhere in the east.

Early European Theories

The first whites who heard these stories viewed them as simplistic fables and dismissed them out of hand. And thereafter, European scholars searched for what they saw as more credible explanations for the origins of the Indians. Dozens of theories appeared in the 1500s and 1600s. Because the authors of these theories believed that the "cradles" of civilization were in or near Europe and the Mediterranean Sea, they almost always envisioned migrations from that region.

For instance, one common thought was that the Indians were descended from Phoenicians or Carthaginians. The Phoenicians were skilled sailors from what is now Palestine who established extensive trade routes across the Mediterranean world in the first millennium B.C. One of their colonies, Carthage, in North Africa, eventually grew into a rich and mighty empire. Some sixteenth-century scholars contended that a number of Phoenician or Carthaginian sailors ventured too far out into the Atlantic and ended up in the Americas. And over time their descendants had become the Indians. Other similar theories suggested that sailors from Egypt, Wales, or other regions of the "Old World" had gone off

course and founded the "New World" populations.

All of the scholars and writers who tried to explain the origins of the Indians were devout Christians. So it is not surprising that many of them turned to the Bible for inspiration. In 1567, for example, a Dutch theologian named Joannes Lumnius revisited the mystery of the lost tribes of Israel. According to the Bible, he pointed out, an Assyrian king had conquered the northern kingdom of Israel and carried away its people to what is now Iraq.[7] These Jews, members of ten early Jewish tribes, never returned to Palestine. So what became of them? According to Lumnius, they somehow made their way across the Atlantic to the Americas, and their descendants became the Indians.

Numerous other Europeans accepted this idea and offered "proof" for it. One was a Portuguese traveler, Antonio Montezinos, who wrote, "It was a thrilling journey I took in South America. Now that I am back . . . I must share with you some incredible news. There is a Jewish Indian tribe living beyond the mountain passes of the Andes [Mountains]. Indeed, I myself . . . saw them observe the Jewish rituals."[8] The rituals that Montezinos claimed he witnessed were never verified. But for centuries to come many Europeans continued to accept a Jewish ancestry for the Indians.

In fact, this notion survives today in Mormon beliefs. According to the Mormon scriptures (*The Book of Mormon*), the Jews who migrated to the Americas split into two groups—the Nephites

An Indian View of the Creation

According to the Chelan Indians of Washington State, the powerful supernatural being known as the Great Chief built the world and fashioned the major kinds of animals. Later, he instructed the wolf brothers to kill the beaver who lived in the water and divide his body into twelve pieces, which would become the first groups of human beings. The youngest of the wolf brothers succeeded in slaying the beaver. Then:

Youngest Brother gave other pieces to other animal people and told them where to go. They took the liver to Clearwater River, and it became the Nez Perce Indians. They took the heart across the mountains, and it became the Methow Indians. Other parts became the Spokane people, the Lake people, the Flathead people. Each of the eleven pieces became a different tribe. "There have to be twelve tribes," said Youngest Brother. "Maybe the Creator thinks that we should use the blood for the last one. Take the blood across the Shining Mountains and wake it up over there. It will become the Blackfeet. They will always look for blood."

Indigenous Peoples' Literature, "Chelan Creation Myth: Creation of the First Indians." www.indians. org/welker/firstind.htm.

This Apache girl has been painted with white clay mixed with sacred corn meal in preparation for her Sunrise Dance, a reenactment of part of the creation myth story.

and Lamanites. Because the Lamanites were evildoers, God cursed them and turned their skins dark. The Nephites, whose skins remained white, were eventually wiped out by the Lamanites, who became the American Indians.

Another theory that invoked biblical traditions to explain the origins of the Indians also involved the lost continent of Atlantis. Atlantis was supposedly a large land mass that existed in the Atlantic Ocean before it sank beneath the waves in a huge catastrophe in ancient times. In 1535 a Spanish writer named Fernandez de Oviedo proposed that after the great flood mentioned in the Bible, the descendants of Noah, builder of the ark, settled in Atlantis. Later, when that continent sank, a few of the inhabitants survived. They then made their way to the nearby Americas, where they established the various Indian tribes.

Asian Migrants?

It is interesting to note that the true explanation for the Indians' origins first appeared in the same period as the more fanciful ones. An earnest and bright Jesuit missionary, José de Acosta, traveled to the Americas in the mid-1500s and lived among the natives for many years. After much careful thought, in 1589 he published his *Natural and Moral History of the Indians*. It contains a theory about the peopling of North America that no one else had considered, namely that the Indians had originated in eastern Asia.

Acosta first considered the animal species of Asia and North America. He saw that several of the same species existed on both continents and concluded that the beasts of one continent must have migrated there from the other continent. This meant that the two land masses must be connected at some spot. (At the time, most of North America and northeastern Asia had yet to be explored by Europeans. So the existence of such a connection seemed at least possible.) Furthermore, Acosta said, if animals could migrate from one land mass to the other, so could people. "We may easily infer from these arguments," he wrote,

that the first Indians went to inhabit the Indies [i.e., North America] more by land than by sea. Or if there were any navigation, it was neither great nor difficult [since] the one world [continent] is continued and joined with the other, or at the least they approach nearer unto another in some parts.[9]

Gradually, Acosta said, the Indians moved from Asia into North America and spread across the continent.

For a long time, Acosta's theory of the Indians' origins remained merely one of many that were proposed and debated in European scholarly circles. Few people accepted it, partly because it presupposed that the native peoples of North America were very ancient. It was more fashionable in those days to suggest that the Indians were offshoots of European peoples, which required their arrival in the Americas to be a fairly recent event.

French Jesuit missionaries preach to Native Americans. One Jesuit, José de Acosta, lived among the Native Americans for years in the mid-1500s and formulated theories about their origins.

The Emergence of Beringia

Over time, however, more and more scientists suspected that the Native Americans were a much older people than had been previously thought. Prominent among them was scholar Samuel Haven of the American Antiquarian Society. In 1856 he published an important study titled *Archaeology of the United States*. Like Acosta, Haven looked toward Asia for

Origins of the American Indians ■ 19

the original homeland of the earliest Indians. "All their characteristic affinities [traits and habits]," Haven wrote, "are found in the early conditions of Asiatic races."[10] These words were written more than a century after Russian explorer Vitus Bering had discovered the strait named for him, lying between Alaska and Siberia. Because he had shown that no land bridge exists between them, most scholars found the idea of an ancient migration from Asia to North America hard to believe. And they gave Haven's proposal about the Indians a cool reception.

Yet Acosta and Haven were eventually proved right. By the 1960s enough geological evidence had been found to ver-

Ancient hunters use bows and arrows to hunt prehistoric mammoths. Remains of such mammoths in Alaska and Canada prove that these animals migrated over a land bridge that existed where the Bering Strait is now.

ify that 18,000 years ago (16,000 B.C.) sea levels were some 300 feet (91m) lower than they are today. Where the Bering Strait now exists, there was a stretch of exposed continental shelf thousands of square miles in extent—now called both the Bering Land Bridge and Beringia. The most recent evidence suggests that Beringia first appeared about 75,000 years ago, during the last major ice age. It shrank considerably during a warming trend lasting from about 40,000 to 25,000 years ago. But then it expanded once more and remained in place until roughly 11,000 years ago.

In the period lasting from about 18,000 to 12,000 years ago, Beringia was largely a subarctic wilderness with few trees. But it had enough small plants, grasses, and freshwater rivers and ponds to sustain small populations of large animals. Among the beasts that evidence now confirms traveled from eastern Siberia, across the land bridge, and into what are now Alaska and Canada were mammoths, huge, woolly, elephant-like creatures. Other imposing animals that dwelled in Beringia included ground sloths 20 feet (6m) long, beavers the size of black bears, bison with horns 6 feet (2m) long, along with camels, reindeer, horses, bears, mountain lions, and wolves.

Treks into New Hunting Grounds

Thus, the very conditions that Acosta long ago envisioned—an expanse of land bridging Asia and North America and migrations of large animals across that expanse—did in fact exist at one time. His assumption that early humans crossed the land bridge, too, was at last a compelling idea that could not be ignored. The exact date of the migration is uncertain. But a good deal of evidence indicates that it did occur. Also, it appears to have taken place within a certain general time frame—between fifteen thousand and eleven thousand years ago.

First, the remains of sites occupied by ancient hunter-gatherers have been found both in eastern Siberia and Alaska. One of the main Siberian sites is a cave at Diuktai on the Middle Aldan River. Like other Siberian sites, it contains not only bones from butchered animals but also stone tools characteristic of these hunters—small, sharpened stone blades used as spear points and knives. Archaeologists refer to them as "microblades." Nearly identical kinds of microblades have been found in ancient sites in the Tanana Valley, 60 miles (97km) southeast of Fairbanks, Alaska, and at other Alaskan sites. Clearly, people from the same Stone Age culture occupied all these sites.

The dating of these sites is also striking because it sets up a believable scenario for the hunters' eastward migration. The Diuktai Cave site dates from about 18,000 years ago. The Alaskan sites range in age from about 13,700 to 11,000 years ago. This suggests that some of the bands of Asian hunters reached Beringia by perhaps 15,000 years ago and that some of their descendants began moving into Alaska about a millennium later.

Dating the Stone Age Siberians

Studies and excavations by archaeologists suggest that northeastern Siberia was not settled by Stone Age hunter-gatherers until eighteen thousand years ago or thereafter. This means that their descendants could not have crossed into North America until a still later date. University of California scholar Brian M. Fagan elaborates:

It seems increasingly likely that no one lived in northeastern Siberia—an arctic desert unthinkable during the height of the last Ice Age . . . until global warming began after 18,000 years ago. This conclusion effectively limits the date of first settlement of the Americas to after the Ice Age and to later than 18,000 years ago. . . . If this chronology is correct, Alaska and Siberia were still joined by the Bering land bridge, the heart of a sunken continent the geologists call Beringia.

Brian M. Fagan, *The Great Journey: The Peopling of Ancient America*. Miami: University Press of Florida, 2003, p. x.

It is clear that only some of the hunters migrated from region to region; probably small groups followed moving animal herds further eastward or southeastward, while most members of their communities stayed put and lived out their lives. Thus, as scholar Philip Kopper points out, these periodic treks into new hunting grounds were not part of some overriding plan but, rather, random and gradual events. "There is no reason to believe that these people knew where they were going," he says,

or even that they knew they were going anywhere. Beringia should not be seen as just an avenue of transit, but as a place where people lived, some of whom moved on.

The term "migration" mistakenly implies intentional relocation, when actually the pace might have been so slow that each generation of immigrants thought they were simply moving to the next overlook or game-rich valley.[11]

This archaeological evidence is strongly supported by recent studies that compared the physical characteristics and DNA of American Indians to certain Asian inhabitants of Siberia. These studies confirm that the two groups were at one time closely related. The DNA evidence also suggests that the Asian migrants did not all arrive in Alaska at once. Rather, they came in waves over the course of two, three, or four thousand years.

These primitive hunter-gatherers, North America's earliest human immigrants, had no idea, of course, that they were making history. As Fagan puts it, it was

a watershed in human development, a moment to pause and wonder at humanity's startling ability to adapt to the extremes of life on planet Earth. Human beings first evolved in the relatively undemanding tropical environments of Africa, then progressively mastered ever more harsh climates. . . . Eventually they came to the frontiers of a vast continent. Soon they were to wander into the heart of the Americas and explode into a new chapter of human history. [12]

Chapter Two

The Peopling of North America

The exact manner in which the early migrants from eastern Asia and Beringia spread out across North America—in a sense "peopling" it—is forever lost in the mists of time. However, archaeologists and other scholars have pieced together a believable general scenario of how it probably happened. This theory is based on small hidden amounts of evidence left behind by these ancient North Americans. Consisting of tools, weapons, animal bones, and other artifacts, said evidence has been found in Canada, the northeastern sector of the United States, the Great Plains, Texas, the Carolinas, and elsewhere.

Modern experts have adopted a number of standard terms to describe these earliest Native Americans. One is Paleo-Indians. The term *Paleo* (or *Palaeo*) comes from a Greek word meaning "ancient," or "prehistoric." Generally speaking, the earliest Paleo-Indians were the first peoples who settled permanently in North America—possibly between 14,000 and 13,500 years ago—after migrating across Beringia. Most scholars use a cutoff date of about 10,000 years ago (8000 B.C.) for the end of the Paleo-Indian phase. North American cultures that flourished after that date, and up until roughly 1,000 years ago, are generally termed Archaic. (*Archaic* comes from another Greek word meaning "old," but in this terminology Archaic Indians are more recent than Paleo-Indians.)

Scholars also classify these early Native Americans by the kinds of stone tools and weapons they used. In particular, terms such as Clovis and Folsom refer to "points"—sharpened weapon blades attached to the ends of spears or used as hand-knives. The same terms describe the peoples or cultures who used these points. Thus, the Clovis culture consisted of early Paleo-Indians who hunted with a distinctive blade now called the Clovis point. And the Folsom peoples were later Paleo-Indians who used the Folsom point, which was similar to but noticeably different from the Clovis point. Later still, various groups of Archaic Indians used a wide range of points, the shapes of which were dictated by their individual needs.

Another general distinction between the Paleo-Indians and Archaic Indians is the role each played in the peopling of North America (and eventually Central and South America). The Paleo-Indian phase witnessed the spread of Native American hunter-gatherers across the entire continent. Recent evidence suggests that these migrations were remarkably rapid. Clovis sites (i.e., archaeological digs containing Clovis points and other artifacts) have been found in central Texas and dated to ca. 12,900 years ago. This means that bands of Clovis hunters spread from northern Canada to Texas—a distance of at least 2,500 miles (4,020km)—in fewer than a thousand years. In contrast, the long period of Archaic Indian cultures that followed saw fewer migrations. Most Archaic Indians adapted to a particular geographic region and developed distinctive customs within that environmental niche.

The Clovis Hunters

The speed at which the Clovis peoples populated North America is perhaps not so surprising when one considers that they were primarily roving hunters.

Archaeologists study tools such as these spear points to classify early Native American tribes.

Studies of early modern peoples who hunted elephants and other large game were conducted in Africa and other parts of the world in the 1800s and 1900s. These studies revealed that the hunters most often followed the herds, which sometimes ranged over hundreds of square miles. The Clovis hunters must have done the same. Their chief prey seems to have been mammoths, huge animals that likely migrated up to 200 miles (322km) in a given season. Therefore, a single band of hunters following such a herd would have become familiar with a very large amount of territory.

Let us suppose that these hunters remained in that region for one or two generations. Then some of them followed one or two other herds, which migrated 100 or 200 miles (161 or 322km) farther southward or eastward. In this way, the descendants of the original band could have settled in an area 1,000 miles (1,610km) away in only ten or twenty generations. Using a rough figure of 25 years for each generation, that is only 250 to 500 years.

To bring down mammoths, giant sloths, moose, reindeer, and other large prey, these hunters used weapons tipped with their signature stone point. The average Clovis point is about four to six inches (10 to 15cm) long. It is also bifacial, which means that when a hunter used a harder stone to flake (chip) and thereby sharpen the point, he did so on both sides. In addition to displaying numerous flake marks, a typical Clovis point is fluted. The fluting consists of a recessed channel carved into the stone near the bottom of the point. The exact reason for this fluting is uncertain. But most experts think that a hunter laid a narrow, rounded wooden shaft into it and tied the shaft and point together securely. Probably the hunter carried several such small, lightweight, pointed shafts with him while stalking game. He would need only one heavier spear with a groove carved in the top. The hunter could push one of the pointed shafts into the groove and then jab the weapon into his prey. Afterward, he could remove the broken or dulled point from the animal and slip a new pointed shaft onto the end of the spear in preparation for the next stalk.

The Clovis hunters likely used such spears at close range, to stab and finish off large animals that were already wounded or otherwise incapacitated. For initial, long-range strikes, they placed their premade pointed shafts into a more ingenious weapon called an atlatl. (The term *atlatl* is the name given to the weapon by the Aztec Indians of central and southern Mexico. Stone Age hunters in what is now the United States and other parts of the world had a wide range of names for it, but modern scholars came to use the Aztec term for all of them.)

About 18 inches (46cm) long, the atlatl was essentially a throwing stick composed of a wooden handle attached to a wooden socket or groove. The hunter inserted the rear end of a premade pointed shaft into the groove and used a forceful overhand motion to send the sharpened point flying through the air. The atlatl produced

The Solutrean Hypothesis

Although all scholars accept the theory that Siberian hunter-gatherers crossed into Alaska perhaps fourteen thousand years ago, some suggest that in addition a second group of Stone Age people might have entered North America from the east. The so-called Solutrean hypothesis was proposed in 1999 by scholars Dennis Stanford and Bruce Bradley. They contend that the Clovis hunters of the Americas might have borrowed the idea for their projectile points from the ancient European Solutrean culture, whose members fashioned somewhat similar points and produced cave art in France some twenty thousand years ago. It is possible, Stanford and Bradley say, that bands of Solutrean hunters crossed broad patches of pack ice in the North Atlantic and made it into what is now Canada. But critics of the hypothesis say that such an ocean crossing would have been too difficult. They also point out that, outside of projectile points, the Clovis and Solutrean cultures were very different; the Clovis people produced no cave art, for instance.

These rocks were the type used by Native Americans to fashion tools.

considerably more forward momentum than was possible to achieve with the arm alone. This meant that it could fire a point farther than the hunter could throw an ordinary spear and that the point struck the prey with more force.

The damage these weapons could inflict has been revealed by the recently discovered remains of mammoths and other large beasts. The bones of a mammoth slain by Clovis hunters were found in Murray Springs, Arizona, for instance. Another mammoth, the remains of which were discovered at Naco, Arizona, died with eight Clovis points imbedded in its body. It is unknown whether eight hunters each struck the beast once, four hunters each hit it twice, or some other combination. Noted archaeologist George Frison suggests that groups of hunters worked in well-coordinated unison to bag such a large animal. One hunter likely distracted the mammoth, he says, after which two or more hunters unleashed their deadly atlatls. It became vital to develop such teamwork, Frison and other scholars point out, because a beast of this size was of tremendous value to the community. A single mammoth, Brian Fagan points out,

> could provide meat for weeks on end, and, if dried, for much of the winter, too. Hides, tusks, bones, and pelts were used to make household possessions and weapons, for shelter, and for clothing. Precious fat from the internal organs could be melted down and used for cooking and burning in [crude oil] lamps. [13]

Clovis Camps

Though big game kills were valuable to the tribe or community, the Clovis peoples likely also relied on other food sources. Fagan speculates:

> Undoubtedly they took not only big Ice Age species, but medium-sized animals like deer, and small rabbits and other mammals, as well. They must also have explored wild plant foods in spring, summer, and fall, as well perhaps as fish and other aquatic resources when the occasion arose. While the hunting of large mammals was sometimes important, and the people wandered far and wide in search of them, we can be sure that there were many distinctive adaptations to locally plentiful and predictable resources, which are not yet reflected in the archaeological record. [14]

Indeed, the more scholars learn about Clovis culture, the more adaptable, resourceful, and clever its members appear to have been. The high quality of their houses is a case in point. For a long time experts assumed that these ancient hunters lived in caves during settled periods and slept under the stars while on the move. However, in the last decades of the twentieth century evidence came to light showing that at least some of the Clovis peoples lived in sophisticated handmade lodges.

For example, excavations at an eleven-thousand-year-old site in Virginia's Shenandoah Valley revealed the remains

The Deadly Atlatl in Action

In the 1540s a member of the expedition of Spaniard Hernando De Soto, the first European to see the Mississippi River, saw some Native Americans using an atlatl and later described it in writing:

One soldier was wounded with . . . a dart . . . [which] is thrown with a wooden strip [the atlatl]. . . . Our Spaniards had never seen this weapon before that day in any part of Florida through which they had traveled. . . . The strip is of wood two-thirds of a yard in length, and is capable of sending a dart with such great force that it has been seen to pass completely through a man armed with a coat of mail [armor made of metal scales sewn or glued to a heavy jerkin]. In Peru, the Spaniards feared this weapon more than any others the Indian possessed, for the arrows there were not so fierce as those of Florida.

Garcilaso De La Vega, *Florida of the Inca,* trans. John and Jeannette Varner. Houston: University of Texas Press, 1951, p. 597.

Australian aborigines hunt with an atlatl in the 1800s. Native Americans also used atlatls to hunt.

of a semipermanent Clovis camp. From a careful study of the soil, diggers determined that rows of wooden posts, by now rotted away, had long ago been driven vertically into the ground. These posts became the framework for a wattle lodge some 36 feet (11m) long. (Wattle is an interwoven mix of twigs, branches, reeds, and/or other plant materials.) Up to thirty people could have found shelter from the elements in this dwelling, which took the excavators by surprise. "Paleo-Indians weren't *supposed* to put that much effort into a house,"[15] University of Delaware scholar Jay F. Custer remarked after inspecting the site.

The Folsom Age

The Folsom hunters who followed the Clovis peoples in North America almost certainly inherited basic lodge- and tool-making skills from their ancestors. One thing that made the Folsom peoples different was the nature of their weaponry. Folsom points are about two inches (5cm) long, considerably shorter than Clovis points. Most Folsom points are also thinner than Clovis versions, with a symmetrical, leaflike structure. In addition, the fluted groove in a Folsom point usually runs nearly the entire length of the blade.

Still another factor that sets Folsom points apart from the earlier Clovis vari-

This model replicates a Neolithic house. Such permanent structures were used by early Native Americans.

Native Americans hunt bison. Differences in tools used by Native American tribes are due in part to the prey each tribe hunted.

ety is the kinds of animals the Folsom peoples hunted. Almost all the Folsom sites so far uncovered contain the remains of bison rather than mammoths. It appears that the physical differences between Folsom and Clovis points were at least in part related to differences in the prey themselves. Because bison are considerably smaller than mammoths, smaller stone points may have been sufficient to bring down bison.

The transition from mammoth to bison hunting was not a matter of choice for the Paleo-Indians. Approximately 12,900 years ago, right at the close of the Clovis period, many of the large Ice Age mammals, including the mammoth and giant sloth, went extinct. At first, scholars were unable to explain how these so-called "megafauna" disappeared so abruptly. Then, in the 1960s Professor Paul Martin of the University of Arizona proposed a new theory. The Stone Age hunters drove these beasts to extinction, he said, by killing large numbers of them in a relatively short span of time.

This "overkill hypothesis" seemed believable at first. But over time a number of experts came to see it as only one of several factors that wiped out the megafauna. Another, some evidence has revealed, was a series of major fluctuations in climate; for example, the end of the Ice Age brought both rising temperatures and periodic serious droughts, which the larger animals were increasingly unable to cope with.

Still another possible factor came to light in 2007. University of Oregon archaeologists Douglas J. Kennett and Jon M. Erlandson announced they had found evidence that a natural disaster had ended the Clovis age. A small comet or large meteor struck the glaciers then covering the region just north of the Great Lakes, they said. The proof consists of a carbon-rich layer found at a certain level in the soil at more than fifty separate Clovis sites. "Highest concentrations of extraterrestrial impact materials occur in the Great Lakes area and spread out from there," Kennett states.

> It would have had major effects on humans [as well as the larger animals]. Immediate effects would have been in the North and East, producing shockwaves, heat, flooding, wildfires, and a reduction and fragmentation of the human population.... This was a massive continental scale, if not global, event.[16]

This extraterrestrial impact theory has yet to be accepted by the majority of North American archaeologists. And even if the catastrophe did occur as proposed, it may not have been the only cause of the transition from the Clovis era to the Folsom age. In any case, what-

ever factor or combination of factors *was* responsible, the end product was the same. The Folsom hunters proved highly adept at bagging bison, deer, and a wide variety of other animals. They also foraged for berries, roots, and other plant products they found growing wild in the areas in which they settled. As a result of this natural abundance, some evidence suggests, local populations of Folsom peoples increased and prospered.

Regional Diversification

Then came a much larger transition with more lasting results. Around ten thousand years ago, major climatic changes occurred that brought about the end of the Paleo-Indian phase and the opening of the long era of the Archaic Indians. University of Arizona scholar Arrell M. Gibson summarizes the environmental changes that caused Indian cultures to become more specific to region and different from each other:

> The glacial ice cap retreated northward. The weather all over North America changed drastically as the climatic patterns we know today with regional variations began to emerge. Thus, the great integrating force of rather constant, continent-wide, mild climate, which had produced a homogeneous [more or less uniform] Paleo-Indian culture, faded. While the eastern portion of North America remained humid and well-watered, arid plains and deserts formed in the central and western sections. This evolving region-

Early Hunters Butcher Bison

Large mammals, including bison, were undoubtedly important mainstays of the diets of Archaic Indians. And these early hunters developed systematic and highly efficient methods of butchering the animals' carcasses. After studying the remains of about two hundred bison killed by hunters in southeastern Colorado some eighty-five hundred years ago, archaeologist Joe Ben Wheat described the butchering process:

The first step was to arrange the legs of the animal so that it could be rolled onto its belly. The skin was then cut down the back and pulled down on both sides of the carcass. . . . Directly under the skin of the back was a layer of tender meat, "the blanket of flesh." When this was stripped away, the bison's forelegs and shoulder blades could be cut free, exposing the highly prized "hump" meat, the rib cage, and the body cavity and its prized organs. Having stripped the front legs of meat, the hunters threw the still articulated bones [away]. If they followed the practice of later Indians, they would next have indulged themselves by cutting into the body cavity, removing some of the internal organs, and eating them raw. . . . What is certain is that the hunters did remove and eat the tongues of a few bison at this stage of the butchering.

Quoted in Philip Kopper, *The Smithsonian Book of North American Indians*. New York: Harry N. Abrams, 1986, pp. 44–45.

al climatic variation produced ecological alterations. Swamps and bogs dried up. The coarse savanna grasses which had sustained the mammoth . . . were replaced by shorter grasses that favored the smaller bison, antelope, deer, elk, and other species familiar today.[17]

Archaic Indians became highly skilled at hunting these and other small animals, as well as catching fish in lakes and ocean inlets. Evidence suggests that most of these peoples supplemented their meat supplies by foraging for plants more so than the Paleo-Indians had. And it was probably increased knowledge of and experimentation with plants that led to the discovery of agriculture in the Archaic period. Not all Indian groups became farmers. And of those who did, some came to rely on their crops more than others. Also, agriculture was often a supplement to hunting and gathering, which remained important sources of food.

The exact manner in which agriculture developed in the Americas and the dates in which farming appeared in various regions is unknown. But it is certain that, once people acquired knowledge of planting seeds and harvesting crops, they began growing vegetables. Cultivation of maize (a kind of corn) and/or squash, beans, and pumpkins had become commonplace in what is now Mexico by perhaps 7,500 years ago; the American southwest by 5,500 years ago; and the eastern United States by 3,000 years ago.

The Archaic period therefore witnessed the Indians of North America branch out into many regional groups and tribes, each of which adopted the food-producing customs that best fit local conditions. Diversification occurred in other cultural areas, too, including spoken languages. By the eve of contact with white Europeans, at least two hundred distinct languages were spoken in North America. Thus, no two Indian groups were the same. And the most effective way to examine their cultures is by region.

Chapter Three

Indians of the American West

Native American groups continued to migrate from region to region during the long Archaic period of North American Indian civilization and even well after it. For example, as late as the A.D. 300s and 1400s, not long before the arrival of the Spanish, long-range migrations of Apache peoples were in progress. The Apache, who ended up in the region of the southwestern United States, originated in Canada. Over the course of perhaps two or three centuries, they moved southward, perhaps through the Great Plains or the foothills of the Rocky Mountains, or both. (Scholars remain unsure.)

Overall, however, such long-range migrations were uncommon in North America in late Archaic times and beyond. Most Indian groups stayed put in a given region, although they might sometimes move their villages or camps from one part of that region to another. Over time, each group quite naturally

adapted to the peculiar terrain, climate, plants, and animals of its native region. This created many regional variations in such areas as food-gathering and hunting, house-building materials and techniques, and craft specialties. Trade and cultural exchange between regions did exist and was sometimes extensive. Yet the many Indian groups had their own distinctive languages and customs and, with occasional exceptions, saw themselves as separate peoples.

In fact, a number of separate Native American peoples, sometimes called tribes, developed in each of the four major geographical regions of what became the United States—the West, Great Plains, Southeast, and Northeastern Woodlands. The reason for this variation within regions is that each major region consists of several subregions. The West, for instance, includes three large subregions—the Northwest Coast, the Far West, and the Southwest. Each

This nomadic tribe uses a horse-pulled travois to tote their belongings. Many Native American tribes were nomadic, and moved according to the season.

subregion then further breaks down into more localized regions. Thus, the Far West consists of the Great Basin (most of Utah and Nevada), California, and the high plateau country of inland Oregon, Washington, and Idaho. Considering the wide variety of distinctive terrains and climates that exist within these subregions, the stunning diversity of local Indian cultures is hardly surprising.

Tribes of the Northwest Coast

Certainly among the more distinctive of these cultures is that of the tribes of the Northwest Pacific Coast region. The area consists of a strip of well-forested territory between 100 and 200 miles (160–320km) wide bordering the ocean and running from southern Oregon up into Canada. Summers there tended to be rather cool, while winters were mild and wet. The plentiful rainfall in most years made the forests in the area dense and lush, producing large numbers of plants to eat or build with. And these same woodlands were crawling with animal species—deer, elk, bears, raccoons, rabbits, and many others—to hunt. At the same time, the nearby sea contained whales, seals, salmon, trout, shellfish, and other creatures that the local natives hunted or

Cleverly Fashioned Log Boats

The Nootka, Haida, and some other peoples of the Pacific and Canadian Northwest learned to make large, sturdy boats, which they launched into the ocean to hunt marine animals, including whales, seals, and fish of all sizes. Many of these vessels were essentially huge redwood or red cedar logs that had been hollowed out and cleverly shaped and tooled to make them seaworthy. First, the boat makers felled the huge trees, usually by controlled burning techniques. Then they split the enormous logs by hammering stone wedges into them. Using both stone tools and controlled burning, they hollowed out a log, thereby producing the basic frame of a boat. To make sure that the hull and other sections were of appropriate and even thickness—so that the vessel would be balanced and maneuverable—the boat makers drilled holes of specific desired depths in various spots from the outside. They then carved away the thicker parts of the inner hull until they reached the holes. And finally they plugged the holes. Some of these boats were sixty feet (18m) long and held more than a dozen hunter-fishermen, plus their catches.

A large log has been shaped into a dugout canoe. Several tribes used this technique.

trapped. "There are few places in the world," the late American archaeologist Gordon Willey remarked, "where land and sea combine to offer such a rich and regular bounty for human consumption, and the Indians of the Northwest Coast . . . exploited it to the full." [18]

The region's tribes included, among many others, the Makah, Chinook, Salish, and Nootka. A great deal is known about the lives and habits of these peoples—more than about ancient Indians in many other parts of the country—in part because of a very fortunate discovery made in 1969. It consists of the remains of an entire Makah town located at Ozette on Washington's Olympic Peninsula. About five hundred years ago, a devastating mud slide buried the town, preserving many of its contents. So far, more than fifty thousand artifacts have been found on the site, including baskets, wooden storage boxes, fishing nets, weapons, dishes, combs, hats, carved figurines of animals and boats, and numerous others.

These and finds made at other Northwest Coast sites show, among other things, how the ancient inhabitants obtained their food. Agriculture was not widespread in the area in large part because of the abundance of animals that were hunted and wild plants that were foraged. The men used wooden slats to build rectangular fishing traps, which they submerged in the ocean or in lakes or streams. They also caught fish in nets and cleverly imbedded rows of sharpened sticks in streams to impale migrating salmon. In addition, hunters paddled wooden boats out into the ocean and hurled razor-sharp harpoons to kill whales and seals. Not all fish were eaten. People burned certain extremely oily fish like candles to provide light after the sun went down; appropriately, these later

These shelters are built from driftwood logs and are covered in dirt and sod. Such dwellings were used by the Yup'k and Cup'tk tribes in Alaska. Many Native Americans used materials from the forest for their dwellings.

came to be called candlefish. Meanwhile, women gathered basketfuls of strawberries, blueberries, elderberries, and other tasty, nutritious plants from nearby forests.

The forests also provided wood and other building materials for remarkably large, sturdy houses. The houses at Ozette and many other northwestern native sites stood in well-organized rows, usually facing the beach. They were made of huge logs stacked horizontally and notched at the ends to fit snugly together. The inside walls were faced with cedar planks. Multifamily dwellings each had a spacious central room with one or more stone hearths (used for fireplaces) shared by all, along with wooden platforms that rose in tiers around it. Separated from one another by wooden screens or woven mats, these upper areas were for sleeping and other private functions.

The structure of the houses at Ozette also reflected the residents' wide differences in social status. The highest-ranking member of a household slept on the highest platform, for instance, and clan heads and members of the families of chiefs had more authority, rights, and privileges than ordinary people. Status was also defined by degree of wealth, including the amount of possessions one owned or land one controlled. High-ranking people, especially chiefs, flaunted their wealth and status through large-scale celebrations called potlatches. In a potlatch, which could last for days, the guests feasted while the host impressed them by distributing loads of valuable goods among them. His stature

was measured "by the grandness of his hospitality," Kopper explains.

Not only did he provide vast amounts of food, but he tested his guests' worthiness by their ability to consume [in] a kind of competition. Huge ceremonial bowls—sometimes boats—were filled with delicacies such as salmon roe or berries preserved in fish oil. Then the guest's party would be challenged to eat it all or lose stature before the other guests and be humiliated by the host.[19]

The Great Basin and High Plateaus

In comparison to the large houses, abundant resources, and accumulated individual wealth common in the Northwest Coast region, the Indians of the Great Basin lived in material simplicity. This is because the rugged mountains and plains of Nevada and Utah were relatively arid and supported far fewer forests and large game. Therefore, the tribes of the Great Basin, including, among others, the Ute, western Shoshone, Paiute, and Washoe, hunted mostly small game.

The highlight of this activity was the annual rabbit hunt, which the first whites in the area witnessed and recorded. Hunters from several native families pieced together an enormous net made of plant fibers. A mix of men, women, and children then used sticks to beat the ground and sagebrush, inducing the rabbits to run toward the net, where the

This fishing weir, using a centuries-old design of woven willow and alder branches, traps fish in the stream above the weir. Early Native American tribes caught fish in a similar fashion.

hunters used clubs to dispatch the animals. Afterward, there was a feast and a celebration.

Then the tribe split up into individual units of one or two families to make foraging for food easier. The families moved from place to place within the Great Basin collecting berries, nuts, and other plant products as they became available at varying times of the year. These seasonal travels "were carefully orchestrated," one scholar writes. "They were nomads not only in the horizontal plane

but also in the vertical, taking advantage of the mountains' various ecological zones. Piñon pine nuts collected in large quantities grew at about 5,000 to 6,000 feet." [20]

One exception to this strictly hunter-gatherer existence was the so-called Fremont culture. Composed of tribal units that are now difficult to identify, they flourished in parts of the Great Basin for about seven hundred years beginning circa A.D. 500. The Fremont peoples grew maize to supplement their hunting and

The World's Finest Baskets?

The Pomo people of northern California developed basket-making skills to the level of high art, and skills that developed millennia ago were passed down through the generations to historic times. The late, great archaeologist and anthropologist Alfred L. Kroeber (1876–1960), studied the Pomo and commented on their distinctive basketry:

Pomo baskets have the name according to many of being the finest in the world. Evidently basket manufacture is no mere utilitarian routine to them, in which they have settled into mechanical habits like other tribes, but an art, the mastery of which is a stimulus and whose possibilities are played with. The height of this display is reached in the basket whose entire exterior is a mass of feathers perhaps with patterns in 2 or 3 lustrous colors. To the Pomo, these served as gifts and treasures, and above all, they were destroyed in honor of the dead. It is impressive and representative of the gently melancholy sentiments of the Pomo that these specimens of the highest artistic achievement of their civilization were dedicated to the purposes of mourning their kindred.

Quoted in "Pomo Baskets for Gifts and Ceremonies." www.kstrom.net/isk/art/basket/pomo.html.

A Pomo basket made in 1905 is decorated with woodpecker and quail feathers and pieces of shell.

foraging. They lived in houses similar to those common in the Southwest, which has led some scholars to propose that they migrated from that region into the basin.

Meanwhile, in the high plateaus lying north of the Great Basin, tribes such as the Yakama, Spokane, Cayuse, Chinookan, and Nez Perce developed a very different lifestyle. These plateaus are heavily forested in some areas. So the natives were fortunate to have a varied menu of wild game, including deer, antelope, elk, beaver, rabbits, and numerous species of birds. Also, the chief rivers in the region—the Columbia and the Fraser—were full of salmon, which the Indians captured as the fish traveled in large numbers to spawn each year. A wide variety of fishing methods were used, including hook and line (with bone hooks), nets, spears, harpoons, nooses, and wooden traps.

California's Diverse Native Peoples

Lying directly west of the Great Basin and south of the Northwest Coast region is California, itself composed of numerous subregions, each with a distinctive terrain and climate. Many of these habitats possess plentiful natural resources. This attracted early migrating people to the region and stimulated population growth among those who settled there. "Aboriginal California was biotically rich, densely populated, and culturally diverse," states University of Oregon scholar Melvin Aikens, "more so than any comparable area of North America."[21]

Indeed, the tremendous diversity of the California tribes, among them the Wintun, Yuki, Miwok, Pomo, Kato, and Chilula, can be seen in the wide array of food sources they exploited. Indians in California's southeastern deserts subsisted, or survived, on mesquite (small spiny trees and bushes in the pea family), beans, and cactus fruits; inhabitants of the semiforested central valleys hunted deer and small game and gathered acorns; people living along the coast caught seals and fish and collected shellfish; and mountain folk hunted deer and wild goats and gathered pine nuts. Also, some primitive planting strategies developed in central California, where the natives raised oaks to produce acorns and cultivated prickly pear cactus to obtain its fruit.

For reasons that are unclear, the early Indian peoples of California did not develop strong tribal political organization and wealth-based social divisions as did their neighbors on the northern coasts. Instead, most California natives broke down into subtribal units, each consisting of a few families. Modern scholars sometimes describe these units as "tribelets." "There was a high degree of isolation among different tribelets," researcher Carl Waldman points out, "with little movement of peoples once the group was established."[22] This unique social structure apparently discouraged intertribal warfare like that seen in many other parts of North America. Although some conflicts must have arisen from time to time, the California native communities usually coexisted in peace.

An illustration depicts an early North American rancheria located in Northern California in the 1800s. Native Americans in California often lived in small, permanent settlements.

During these long periods of peace, various California Indian communities developed craft skills of an extremely high level. Of particular note were the baskets woven by the Pomo, who lived in the area north of San Francisco Bay. These artifacts rank among the most beautiful examples of that art from any society in world history. Fortunately, the intricate techniques involved passed from generation to generation among Pomo women, and their descendants were still producing magnificent baskets in the twentieth century.

The Prosperous Southwestern Peoples

Strong craft skills and traditions also developed in the Southwest, the region lying east of Southern California and including what are now Arizona, New Mexico, and parts of neighboring states. In this case, the leading craft was ceramics, or pottery making. Most of

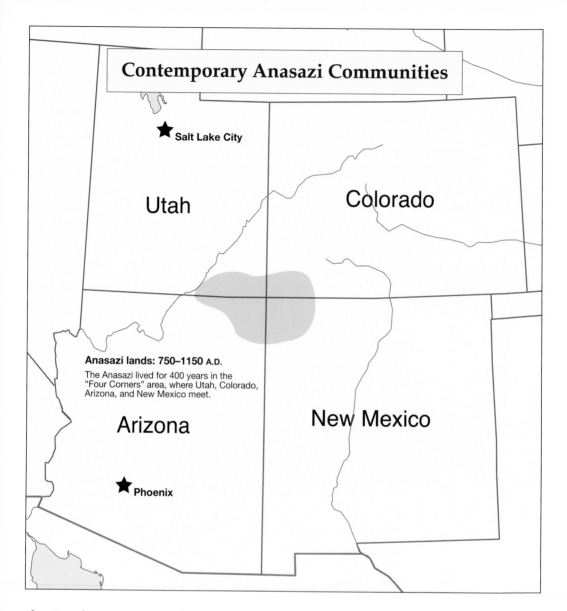

Contemporary Anasazi Communities

★ Salt Lake City

Utah

Colorado

Anasazi lands: 750–1150 A.D.

The Anasazi lived for 400 years in the "Four Corners" area, where Utah, Colorado, Arizona, and New Mexico meet.

Arizona

New Mexico

★ Phoenix

the Southwestern peoples made pottery by manipulating wet clay and then using either sunlight or fire to harden it. They painted the hardened clay with brushes made from the fibers of the yucca plant. Especially impressive were the ceramic containers made by the Mogollon peoples of New Mexico's Mimbres River valley.

The region in which these and neighboring tribes lived was and remains arid and rugged. Terrains range from flat, hot deserts in the south to high, windswept plateaus in the north, punctuated in various places by deep canyons and clusters of stony mountains. As was the case with other Archaic Indians, the residents of this region were at first hunter-gatherers.

However, in time they developed a large-scale agricultural system that produced huge quantities of maize, beans, and squash. Several of the local tribes also grew cotton and used the fibers to make clothes. Among these peoples were the Havasupai (who lived inside the Grand Canyon), Walapai, Yuma, Pima, Mohave, Hopi, and Zuni. The Apache and Navajo arrived much later than the others after migrating from the north.

Scholars suspect that some of these southwestern tribes, including the Hopi, were descended from a very successful earlier people. They are most often referred to today as the Anasazi (the Navajo name for them). The Anasazi lived atop the region's northern plateau (in the so-called "Four Corners" area) in late Archaic times and developed effective farming techniques, including elaborate irrigation systems that diverted water from rivers and creeks to fields. For reasons still not well understood, their numbers increased substantially after A.D. 700. And for several centuries they enjoyed increasing prosperity.

At first the Anasazi lived in pit houses, round structures partly buried underground, with dome-shaped roofs made of wattle. People entered through a hole in the ceiling and climbed down a ladder. Over time they expanded these dwellings by adding walls made of

Pima Indians eke out a living in the desert southwest in the 1800s.

adobe (mud brick) aboveground. And houses, storerooms, and communal centers (large round chambers called kivas) grew more numerous and interconnected until they formed a large complex called a pueblo. The builders grouped "the rooms together with shared walls and on top of one another, ladders connecting the various levels," Waldman explains. "With the levels stepped back in terraces, the roofs of one could serve as the front yards of another below."[23]

The golden age of the pueblos roughly spanned the period of A.D. 1100 to 1300. The Anasazi became extremely prosperous, and their techniques of building, farming, weaving, and pottery making spread outward across neighboring areas of the Southwest. So did their religious rites, which were a vital aspect of their culture. Pueblo society was highly dependent on farming, especially growing corn to feed its large population. And elaborate religious rituals evolved to ensure sufficient rain and abundant harvests. According to Gibson:

> The annual opening of the irrigation ditches, the harvest, rain-making pageants—all were occasions for

Similarities Among Indian Religions

The details of Native American religion varied from region to region and often tribe to tribe. They "had different views of the supernatural world," New York State Historical Association researcher Carl Waldman points out, "with varying types of deities and spirits . . . lore concerning the creation and structure of the universe, [and] an array of rites, ceremonies, and sacred objects." However, most Indian groups did have certain basic religious ideas in common. For example, according to University of Oklahoma scholar Arrell M. Gibson, their "universe was directed by an omnipotent creative-directive force, and the physical environment was alive with various spirits, good and bad, which had to be placated [appeased] in order to succeed in various enterprises. One's clan association provided a supernatural link with an animal ancestor, which related one to all living things." Waldman adds: "Shamanism was a common form of religious practice, in which individuals sought to control these spirits through the use of magic." Other similarities between Indian religions included "the quest for visions [to make contact with the spirits], and the use of psychotropic [mind-altering] plants to facilitate those visions; music and dance as a part of ritual; and the notion of sacrifice to gain the favor of the gods or spirits."

Carl Waldman, *Atlas of the North American Indian*. New York: Facts On File, 1985, p. 57; Arrel M. Gibson, *The American Indian: Prehistory to the Present*. Lexington, MA: D.C. Heath, 1980, pp. 54–55.

The Cliff Palace is an ancient Anasazi cultural settlement located in Mesa Verde National Park in Colorado. It was built between 1190 and 1280 A.D.

pueblo religious observance. It is estimated that pueblo men spent at least half of their time in religious activities. Some were private . . . rites in the *kivas*. Some were public ceremonies with colorful costumes, ritual dancing, and chanting.[24]

The annual rains the Anasazi prayed for eventually dissipated, seriously reducing their crop yields. At least this is one of the theories scholars have advanced to explain a strange, still unexplained historical event. Beginning in about 1300, the Anasazi abandoned their pueblos and moved southward and eastward away from their ancestral lands. Other theories for this population displacement include soil erosion and/or deforestation; inva-

sions of warlike intruders, perhaps some of the Apache peoples; or a combination of these factors.

Later, other tribes, including the Hopi, built pueblos in the region. (Hence, they are sometimes called, along with the Anasazi, "Pueblo Peoples.") Their impressive adobe towns and advanced farming techniques amazed the Spanish when they first arrived in the 1500s. And a few pueblos survived into modern times. The Hopi pueblo at Oraibi in northeastern Arizona, still in use today, is the longest continually occupied settlement in the United States. It stands as a testament to the era when the American Southwest supported one of the world's most accomplished and successful premodern civilizations.

Chapter Four

Native Tribes of the Great Plains

The area most often called the Great Plains was an extremely large amount of territory that covered all or parts of at least fifteen future U.S. states, along with portions of southern Canada. From Montana, Wyoming, and Colorado, it stretched eastward through the Dakotas and Missouri and also extended southward into Oklahoma, Texas, and Arkansas. "This vast region," Waldman writes,

> is predominately treeless grassland—the long grass of the eastern prairies, with 20 to 40 inches of rainfall a year; and the short grass of the western high plains, with 10 to 20 inches of rainfall. There are some wooded areas interrupting the fields of grass—stands of mostly willows and cottonwoods along the many river valleys.[25]

Many large animal species were native to these lands, among them white-tailed deer, mountain goats, antelopes, elk, bighorn sheep, bears, wolves, raccoons, and birds. But the region's most noticeable and majestic creature was the bison (or buffalo), tens of millions of which roamed the grasslands.

The bison-dominated Great Plains were at one time or another home to many Indian groups and tribes. Among them were the Arapaho, Cheyenne, Crow, Sioux, Iowa, Mandan, Caddo, Osage, Wichita, Pawnee, and numerous others. These peoples were for a long time a mix of hunter-gatherers and farmers. But eventually some of them nearly gave up hunting in favor of farming, only to return to hunting later. This unusual series of events occurred because the Great Plains was unique among Indian geographic and cultural regions in an important way. Its inhabitants were significantly affected by the horse, which white people had introduced into North America well before the natives of the plains had made contact with white civilization. Horses profoundly changed the customs and history of many of the plains Indians.

Plains Hunters Before the Horse

Both Paleo-Indians and Archaic Indians killed and slaughtered bison and other large animals in the region for millennia, beginning at least twelve thousand years ago. And throughout these periods, such hunts were conducted on foot. Indeed, one common early hunting method was the "foot surround." It consisted of a long line of people who encircled a group of grazing bison and slowly tightened the circle. After two, three, or more of the creatures were surrounded, hunters killed them with spears.

Improvements in such basic techniques, as well as in the effectiveness of hunting weapons, appeared only very slowly and gradually. But each improvement made it easier to kill large prey, which sustained existing hunting societies and promoted further exploitation of the region by both them and newcomers. For example, sometime in the late Archaic period bison corrals came into use. Several animals could be herded into a corral and killed later at

A painting by George Catlin depicts Native Americans riding horses. Horses, brought by whites to North America, significantly changed Native American culture.

the hunters' convenience. What archaeologists call the Ruby corral, located on a tributary of the Powder River in Wyoming, is an excellent example. "The corral bears a surprising resemblance to modern cattle corrals," says Fagan.

The hunters erected pairs of stout posts separated by the diameter of the horizontal timbers wedged between them. The result was a strong structure that could withstand the onslaught [attack] of penned animals. . . . Excavators found bison ribs and jaws that were used for digging the post holes into the soft, sandy soil. The builders used juniper wood, perhaps burning off suitable poles rather than cutting them down. . . . Twenty hunters could have taken between 10 and 14 days to build the Ruby corral.[26]

Another hunting improvement, the Besant point, appeared on the plains in about 300 B.C. Long and dartlike, this projectile blade was more effective against bison than earlier points. Another important weaponry advance was the bow and arrow, which came into use on the plains

Native American hunters drive buffalo off a cliff. This technique was probably used rarely, as it resulted in the death of a lot of animals.

perhaps about A.D. 500. At first it merely supplemented spears and atlatls. But over time a number of tribes made the bow their chief hunting weapon. Its advantages were that arrows shot from bows traveled farther than spears or shafts fired by atlatls, arrows were easier to make and lighter to carry than spears, many arrows could be carried by a single hunter, and arrows were easier and faster to load onto a bow than pointed shafts were onto a spear.

Still another hunting improvement was an increased use of an old strategy that had been employed when possible and practical since late Ice Age times. Later called the "bison jump," it consisted of a band of hunters stampeding a group of bison over a steep bluff or small cliff. Because dozens or even hundreds of the beasts were killed in such a communal hunt, plains hunters probably conducted them infrequently, when certain conditions seemed to warrant them. "For such mass hunting strategies to be successful," Fagan points out,

> the bison density would have had to reach a critical level, a density only reached at certain times of the year, when patterns of animal migration permitted it. Many communal hunts may have been annual affairs, or conducted after periods of higher rainfall . . . when the bison population increased. [27]

Many of these bison hunters eventually settled down in semipermanent camps. Most such settlements were located in the low hills along the western borders of the plains rather than on the grasslands themselves. Commonly, bands of hunters ventured out onto the plains for a few weeks each year. One good hunt could provide enough bison products to meet a settlement's needs for many months; so the residents of each settlement likely conducted such hunts only once, twice, or at most three times a year.

Farmers of the Eastern Plains

However, by the time the bow and arrow appeared, some of these western plains bison hunters regularly killed more beasts than they actually needed to sustain themselves. They traded the extra carcasses to Indians living in the eastern sector of the plains. These eastern plains peoples are often called the Plains Woodland Indians. (They are also sometimes referred to as the Plains Village Indians because they usually lived in permanent villages.) In exchange for the dead bison, they gave their western neighbors bushels of corn, beans, and squash. These crops were the mainstay of the Plains Woodland Indians' diet. They did eat some bison meat, but only as a supplement to vegetables; and they sought the bison carcasses mainly for the hides, sinew (tendon), and bones, which they used for making clothes and tools.

Who were these plains farmers and where did they come from? The answer seems to be that most, including the Mandan, Hidasta, Caddo, Wichita, and Pawnee, had descended from the same Archaic peoples the western plains

Amazingly Skilled Horsemen

Some plains warriors developed the riding of horses to a level far beyond that ever achieved by whites. In his nineteenth-century travels on the plains, noted painter and writer George Catlin observed the amazing riding skills of Comanche warriors, later calling them "the most extraordinary horsemen that I have yet seen in all my travels." According to Catlin's riveting account:

Amongst their feats of riding, there is one that has astonished me more than anything of the kind I have ever seen, or expect to see, in my life . . . by which [a young man] is able to drop his body upon the side of his horse at the instant he is passing, effectually screened from his enemies' weapons as he lays in a horizontal position behind the body of his horse, with his heel hanging over the horse's back; by which he has the power of throwing himself up again, and changing to the other side of the horse if necessary. In this wonderful condition, he will hang whilst his horse is at fullest speed, carrying with him his bow and his shield, and also his long lance of fourteen feet in length, all or either of which he will wield upon his enemy as he passes; rising and throwing his arrows over the horse's back, or with equal ease and equal success under the horse's neck.

George Catlin, *Letters and Notes on the Manners, Customs, and Conditions of North American Indians,* vol. 1. New York: Dover, 1973, p. 321.

This painting by George Catlin shows Comanche Indians practicing feats of horsemanship.

A Pawnee family stands in front of its sod house. Once food sources became more consistent through agricultural and improved hunting techniques, formerly nomadic tribes built more permanent settlements.

Indians had. Thus, the eastern plains peoples had originally been bison hunters who supplemented their diets by foraging for roots, berries, seeds, and other plant products. Sometime between 100 B.C. and A.D. 100, however, knowledge of agriculture filtered into their homelands. And in the centuries that followed, these tribes largely replaced hunting with farming. It eventually became typical for a single Indian farming family to cultivate between 1.5 and 3 acres (0.6–1.2ha); such a plot likely produced from ten to twenty large bushels of vegetables per season.

The need to tend and nurture their farming plots on a nearly full-time basis forced these peoples to abandon their old seminomadic lifestyle and settle down. Indeed, the adoption of permanent settlements became one of the hallmarks of the Plains Woodland Indians. Their villages often featured protective stockades (or animal pens) made of wooden poles. Other customs common to all eastern plains farmers were the use of hoes made from bison shoulder blades and the production of crude but sturdy, round pottery bowls and other vessels.

Still another shared trait of the plains farmers was the use of permanent dwellings, which were often quite large and comfortable. The Wichita and Caddo in the southeastern plains, for example, constructed grass houses. According to one expert, a typical grass house consisted of

a frame of cedar poles arranged conically [cone-shaped], with one end anchored in the ground and the tops bound together with sapling strips. . . . Wheat grass, coarser and denser than regular prairie grass, was lashed to this frame in bunches beginning at the bottom and continuing in overlapping rows to the peak.[28]

Farther north, in the east-central sector of the region, the Mandan and others had earthen lodges. Between 26 and 28 feet (8–8.5m) long, these were rectangular and had sod roofs held up by walls made of tightly spaced wooden poles. An earthen hearth was centrally located for heating and cooking, and the smoke vented away through a hole in the ceiling. Meanwhile, the residents stretched animal hides across the entrances to keep out the cold in winter. About seven to fifteen people lived in each sod house, and an average community supported up to three hundred people or more. Archaeologists have revealed that one early Mandan site on the Missouri River in North Dakota had more than a hundred houses; so the village probably had a population of a thousand or more people.

These farmers rarely moved around. But on occasion, perhaps during periods of drought when harvests were poor, they sent out bands of hunters to bag big animals, especially bison. Like other plains peoples, they transported loads of supplies and dead beasts on pole sledges pulled by teams of dogs. In 1598, on the eve of the introduction of the horse to the plains, a Spanish explorer visited the southern plains and saw these dogs in action. They were "medium sized, shaggy dogs," he later wrote,

> which they harness like mules. They have large droves of them, each girt around the breast and haunches, carrying a load of at least one hundred pounds. They travel at the same pace as their masters. It is both interesting and amusing to see them traveling along, one after the other, dragging the ends of their poles. [29]

The Coming of the Horse

Much of this changed dramatically when the first horses appeared on the Great Plains. It did not happen all at once. Rather, the Spanish brought horses with them in the 1500s when they began exploring New Mexico in the Southwest. At first they carefully guarded their horses, which were very valuable and hard to replace. They even made laws that forbade selling horses to the local southwestern Indians. But over time, these laws were poorly enforced and some Spaniards secretly sold horses to the natives. Also, some Indians stole the animals.

In whatever ways the southwestern Indians acquired horses, they swiftly learned to care for, breed, and ride them. And they began to pass on this knowledge to neighboring tribes. Before ever meeting white people, increasing numbers of plains Indians heard about the fabulous "mystery dogs," as they initially referred to horses. Steadily, horse breeding and the creation of new herds spread eastward and northeastward onto the plains. The Apache, who were still in the process of migrating toward the Southwest, had horses at least by 1640. The Comanche in northern Texas had them by 1700; the Shoshone in Wyoming had them by 1720; the western plains Cheyenne, Arapaho, Crow, Blackfeet, and Sioux had them by 1740; and the

Assiniboin and Cree of the far northern plains had them only a decade or two later.

In historical terms, the horse transformed the lives of these peoples almost overnight. "With horses," Texas Tech University professor Paul H. Carlson explains,

> they could take more bison and animal skins to exchange with traders for blankets, beads, knives, hatchets, [and so on]. Moreover, horses became a significant element in gift-giving—important in plains Indians' concepts of status and rank. Horse ownership became a symbol of a man's skill and bravery, for he had to acquire horses by raiding the enemy or by capturing them in the wild. In short, the horse became the most important vehicle of transportation, medium of exchange, and regulator of economic values and social status. It came to exercise considerable influence over the minds of the people, altering world views, religious practices, subsistence patterns, and even the traditional nature and ideology of warfare.[30]

Plains Indians hunt and kill a buffalo. By using horses to hunt, Native Americans could more consistently find and kill game.

Social Customs Affected by Horse Ownership

As Texas Tech University scholar Paul H. Carlson explains, the acquisition of horses changed the economic and social customs of the plains Indians:

Property wealth, measured in numbers of horses, assumed significance in that a wealthy man must be a successful hunter or warrior. Wealth validated bravery, for through successful hunting and raiding a man obtained new wealth in the form of horses and goods. It also became tied to status in that one might improve one's social position by an unselfish sense of sharing, even to the extent of giving away personal possessions. Moreover, because socioeconomic values emphasized generosity (or *wacantognaka* to the Lakotas, one of their four principal virtues), the more horses one gave away, the higher one rose in the status system.

Paul H. Carlson, *The Plains Indians*. College Station: Texas A&M University Press, 1998, p. 53.

The manner in which horses altered food acquisition and lifestyles on the plains was particularly striking. Some of the farmers of the eastern plains, like the Mandan, retained their fields and crops. But others, including the Pawnee, largely gave up farming and adopted a nomadic existence as mounted bison hunters. Meanwhile, many western plains tribes that had long dwelled on the edges of the vast grasslands now moved out onto the plains and, like the Pawnee, became nomads following the herds.

Emergence of the Horse and Bison Culture

As time went on, these nomadic hunters exchanged ideas and copied one another's customs. Techniques of hunting with the bow and arrow from a moving horse, for example, became the same all across the plains. Also, nearly all the nomadic tribes in the region came to use tepees, cone-shaped tents that could be easily assembled and disassembled, ensuring a group's mobility. In addition, everyone's transport sledges were now pulled by horses rather than by dogs. Therefore a sharing of customs and a sort of blending of plains cultures occurred in the 1700s and early 1800s. Modern scholars sometimes call the resulting mixture the "Composite Plains Culture," although it is more often referred to as the "Horse and Bison Culture."

Another cultural aspect that became increasingly similar across the plains was a set of religious rituals that revolved around supernatural visions experienced by individuals. The belief was that in an altered mental state a person might receive guidance from ancestral spirits. "The search for visions often included isolation and self-torture," Gibson writes.

By punishing the flesh, members believed, one edified the spirit, thus sharpening it, making it more receptive to the vision, which would provide guidance for future actions. Focus of warrior power was the sacred medicine bundle containing [items such as] feathers [thought to possess] supernatural character, all enclosed in a cured otter skin.[31]

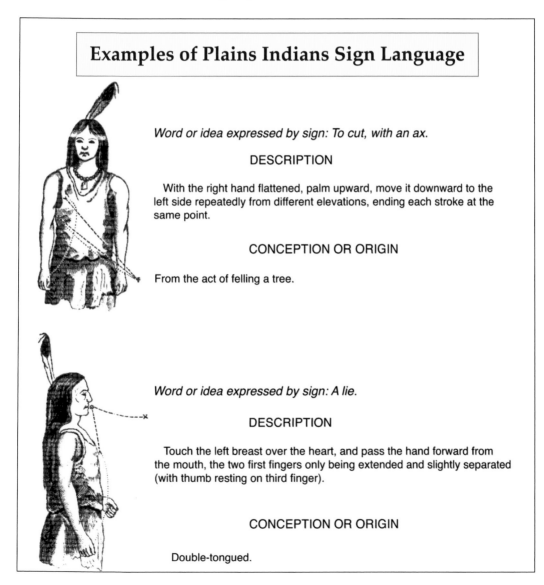

Examples of Plains Indians Sign Language

Word or idea expressed by sign: To cut, with an ax.

DESCRIPTION

With the right hand flattened, palm upward, move it downward to the left side repeatedly from different elevations, ending each stroke at the same point.

CONCEPTION OR ORIGIN

From the act of felling a tree.

Word or idea expressed by sign: A lie.

DESCRIPTION

Touch the left breast over the heart, and pass the hand forward from the mouth, the two first fingers only being extended and slightly separated (with thumb resting on third finger).

CONCEPTION OR ORIGIN

Double-tongued.

Selecting the Most Nutritious Prey

While excavating a bison kill site at Garnsey, New Mexico, archaeologist John Speth of the University of Michigan discovered that American Indian hunters were extremely observant about the physical attributes of their prey and often did not kill bison and other beasts indiscriminately. In the kill he examined, the hunters were selective and went after the male bison. Speth thinks this was because the males are hardier in the spring and that their bone marrow has a higher fat content than that of females at that time of year. The Indians may have preferred fattier meat because it is an important source of energy and certain nutrients.

One cultural trait that individual tribes of the Horse and Bison Culture did not share was language. Each tribe retained its original spoken tongue. Yet these groups frequently came into contact and needed to communicate with one another. So they developed a sign language consisting primarily of hand gestures. Some of the first whites who penetrated the region mistakenly assumed that this sign language had predated the area's spoken languages. But the truth was completely the opposite. This was only one of many misunderstandings and cultural differences between the Indians and whites that would eventually lead all the plains tribes to the brink of extinction.

Chapter Five

Early Inhabitants of the Southeast

While some Native Americans were erecting adobe pueblos in the Southwest and others were hunting bison on the Great Plains, still others had developed an extraordinarily complex and successful lifestyle in what is now the southeastern United States. In the context of precontact Indian civilization, the so-called Southeast was an extremely large region. It included all the territory bordering the Gulf of Mexico, including Louisiana, Mississippi, Alabama, and Florida, as well as Georgia and Tennessee to the north. Some aspects of southeastern Indian culture also extended into the Carolinas, Virginia, and the Ohio River valley. (The peoples of the Ohio Valley were culturally related to the northeastern Indians as well. In fact, archaeologists often group a number of northeastern and southeastern Indian groups together under the label "Eastern Woodlands" Indians.)

Just prior to the arrival of European whites in North America, many separate tribes inhabited the vast Southeast. Among them were the Creeks, Choctaw, Seminole, Cherokee, Chickasaw, Tuskegee, Cusabo, Natchez, and Alabama. Although these tribes occupied numerous different terrains and ecological niches within the Southeast, they all experienced certain similar geographic and climatic conditions. As a whole, the area is well watered, with plentiful rainfall and rich soil, for instance. It also features many low mountain ranges (the largest being the Appalachians) with rolling hills, deep forests, and numerous river valleys. The local Indians lived mostly in permanent villages in these valleys. The vast majority of them were farmers who supplemented their diets by fishing, hunting, and foraging.

It is now known that the tribal identities of most of these local Indian groups were relatively new at the time of first contact with white civilization. Their ancestors had inhabited the area as far back as the Paleo and Archaic eras. But in late Archaic times, a new and quite unique civilization had developed in the Southeast. At its height it featured large political-territorial units, each with a central town and ruled by a high-ranking chief, hence the common modern term "chiefdoms" to describe them.

Even more characteristic of these mini Indian nations was that they erected earthen burial mounds, some of them huge. For that reason, their inhabitants are often called the Mound Builders. Their civilization, which lasted for some twenty-five hundred years, was an intermediary stage between the Archaic Indians of the Southeast and the many localized tribes that formed there after the decline of the large chiefdoms. Many of these southeastern tribes retained the important political, social, and religious customs of the mysterious Mound Builders.

Mystery of the Mound Builders

Most early white explorers lacked a true appreciation for the number and size of the earthworks erected by the Mound Builders. Only when white civilization

Saul's Mound, 72 feet high, is one of the Pinson Mounds, the largest Middle Woodland mound group in the United States. Early white colonists did not believe that Native Americans could build such huge structures.

Jefferson Excavates a Mound

The great American patriot and third U.S. president, Thomas Jefferson, was fascinated by American Indians and their history. In 1782 he excavated a burial mound not far from his Virginia home and later described it:

There being one of these [mounds] in my neighborhood . . . I determined to open and examine it thoroughly. It was situated on the low grounds of the Rivanna [River], about two miles above its principal fork, and opposite to some hills, on which had been an Indian town. It was of a spherical form, of about 40 feet diameter at the base, and had been of about twelve feet altitude [height], though now reduced by the plow to seven and a half feet . . . . I first dug superficially in several parts of it, and came to collections of human bones, at different depths, from six inches to three feet below the surface. These were lying in the utmost confusion, some vertical, some oblique, some horizontal, and . . . entangled, and held together in clusters by the earth. . . . The bones of which the greatest numbers remained were skulls, jaw-bones, teeth, the bones of the arms, thighs, legs, feet, and hands.

Thomas Jefferson, *Notes on the State of Virginia,* chap. 11, American Studies at the University of Virginia. http://xroads.virginia.edu/~hyper/JEFFERSON/ch11.html.

began to spread westward from the eastern seaboard in the late 1700s and early 1800s did whites realize the vast extent and achievements of the mound-building civilization. One of the first writings that called attention to the Mound Builders was Thomas Jefferson's *Notes on the State of Virginia,* published in 1784. Besides being one of the founding fathers of the United States, Jefferson was a versatile individual with interests and broad knowledge in many scholarly disciplines. He was particularly fascinated by Indians and their origins and customs, and he personally excavated a small ancient Indian mound in his native Virginia. The mounds, he wrote,

are of different sizes, some of them constructed of earth, and some of loose stones. That they were repositories of the dead, has been obvious to all. . . . Some have thought they covered the bones of those who have fallen in battles. . . . Some ascribed them to the custom, said to prevail among the Indians, of collecting, at certain periods, the bones of all their dead. . . . Others again supposed them the general [cemeteries] for towns.[32]

Jefferson did not venture a guess about who had built these mounds. He seems to have assumed that ancient Indians had done so, an opinion that was summarily dismissed by the next generation of scholars who studied the mounds. Indeed, in the nineteenth century most whites concluded that these large-scale mounds, especially those 30 feet (9m), 50 feet (15m), and even 100 feet (30.5m) tall, could not be the work of Indians. As James A. Brown of Northwestern University puts it:

> The then prevalent white attitude [was] that Native Americans were too indifferent to labor to have been capable of devoting the effort required in the mounds' construction and would not have had the engineering knowledge to plan and execute the most demanding examples. So entrenched were early [white] Americans in their negative perception of Native American abilities that they paid little attention to any testimony to the contrary. [33]

The testimony that seemed more believable to white researchers and writers was that the mounds had been erected by a "lost" race of whites. The most popular theory was that members of the so-called lost tribes of Israel had erected the mounds. When one educated observer, physician James McCulloh, argued that the Indians' own ancestors had done it, he was ignored or ridiculed.

McCulloh was finally proven right when the newly created federal Bureau of Ethnology thoroughly investigated numerous mounds across the Southeast

between 1881 and 1893. This study, headed by scholar Cyrus Thomas, showed conclusively that the mounds had been built by the not-too-distant ancestors of various Indian tribes in the region. Thus, one important part of the mystery of the Mound Builders had been solved.

The Earliest Mound Builders

The first mounds in the Southeast were likely small piles of earth, each intended to inter a single warrior or chief. And thanks to erosion from rain, wind, floods, and other natural processes, most of these initial mounds are either gone or will never be found. So archaeologists remain unsure when and where the first mounds were erected.

But they all agree that the earliest large-scale example was at Poverty Point, near the confluence of the Arkansas and Mississippi rivers in northern Louisiana. Poverty Point, which flourished roughly between 1700 and 700 B.C., seems to have been a well-organized town shaped like a hemisphere, or giant C. Following the natural curve of the hemisphere are six concentric earthen ridges that measure, on average, 10 feet (3m) tall and 82 feet (25m) wide. They were originally higher and may have supported rows of wooden or wattle houses.

To the west of these ridges lies a huge mound some 66 feet (20m) tall and more than 660 feet (200m) long. The purpose of this mound is uncertain. No human remains have been found in it, so it does not appear to have been for burials. Some experts point out that it is shaped somewhat like a bird, which suggests perhaps that a certain species of bird was sacred to the inhabitants and that the mound had ritual significance and purposes.

Overall, the most striking thing about Poverty Point is its unusual size and lay-out. Its building required a massive amount of organization and cooperation in an age when other Indians in the region were living in tiny, primitive vil-lages. "The Poverty Point habitation cov-ers about 494 acres (200 ha)," Fagan

An aerial view shows the bird-like layout of the ancient village of Poverty Point in northern Louisiana.

Poverty Point's Strategic Location

The reason the builders of Poverty Point, in northern Louisiana, chose that particular spot is unknown. But the late geologist and archaeologist Roger Saucier ventured this guess:

I guess we'll probably never know exactly why [the] Poverty Point people settled exactly where they did. I have a feeling that that is probably largely a matter of socio-economics or perhaps a socio-political factor. But obviously the Poverty Point peoples liked the margins of ridges like Macon Ridge. This has afforded them high ground relatively immune from flooding, with good arable soils and good locations for living conditions. But perhaps more importantly, this enabled them to be immediately adjacent to these very rich bottomland forests and hardwood areas that are so abundant as far as plants and wildlife and fisheries are concerned.

Quoted in Louisiana Office of State Parks, "Poverty Point Earthworks." www.lpb.org/programs/povertypoint/pp_transcript.html.

points out. "[It] took more than 1,236,000 cubic feet (35,000 cu. m) of basket-loaded soil to complete. . . . One authority has calculated that 1,350 adults laboring 70 days a year would have taken three years to erect the earthworks, but the actual permanent population of the site remains unknown." [34]

Though their town was highly unique for its time, the residents of Poverty Point sustained themselves as other southeastern Indians then did—through hunting, fishing, and foraging, supplemented by a little farming. The same was true of the next major group of Mound Builders in the region, called the Adena culture. It was the first mound-building society that spread outward and encompassed numerous settlements in a wide area. Centered in southern Ohio, Adena sites have been found in Kentucky and other nearby states. The Adena culture thrived from about 1000 B.C. to about A.D. 200.

Unlike the Poverty Point earthworks, the Adena mounds, shaped like cones or domes, were mainly for burial. Usually such a mound began when an honored person was buried in a shallow pit and people poured basketfuls of earth over the grave to mark it. Then, over time, other burials were placed atop the bottom one and as a result the mound grew larger and larger. Often mourners placed various goods—including tools, weapons, jewelry, and decorative masks—in the graves along with the bodies. The Adena peoples also constructed nonburial earthworks that experts call effigy mounds. These are frequently shaped like animals, so they may have had religious significance. The most outstanding example is the "Great Serpent Mound" in Peebles, Ohio, shaped like an uncoiling snake and measuring 4 feet (1.2m) high and 1,330 feet (405m) long.

The Highly Successful Hopewells

During the last few centuries in which the Adena culture was building villages attended by burial and effigy mounds, another mound-building culture was rising to prominence in the Southeast. Modern scholars call this newer group of peoples the Hopewell culture. It prospered from about 300 B.C. to roughly A.D. 700. Thus, during this historical overlap, both cultures coexisted for a while, though the extent and nature of their relationship is unclear.

More certain is that the Hopewells and Adenas were quite similar in a number of ways and that the Hopewell culture was based on Adena culture. However, the Hopewells created what might be called a more elaborate, mature, and spectacular version of Adena civilization. The Hopewells built more and larger mounds than the Adenas did, for example. And Hopewell culture spread over a much larger area, stretching from the Gulf of Mexico northward into the Great Lakes region. (Thus, the Hopewells influenced the cultures of a number of later northeastern tribes, too.) The Hopewells also developed a more extensive agricultural system and more varied and impressive craft and artistic works.

The latter included copper earrings, breastplates, and animal figurines; pearl jewelry; obsidian knives and spearheads; small containers made from marine shells; figurines, mirrors, and geometric decorations made from thin sheets of mica; and pottery jars (in a style sometimes referred to as "Hopewell Series"). These and a great many other artifacts were either manufactured in Hopewell towns or obtained through trade. Indeed, trade was especially important to the Hopewells, who exchanged goods with other native peoples across nearly the entire eastern United States.

The most spectacular artifacts of Hopewell culture, however, were the many mounds its people erected. Often they were grouped in enormous complexes. At Chillicothe in the Ohio River valley, for instance, thirty-eight mounds were built within an enclosure covering 110 acres (45ha). And at Newark, Ohio, a complex of mounds and other earthworks covers an area of more than 4 square miles (10.4 sq. km). On average, the larger Hopewell mounds are some 30 feet (9m) high and some are as tall as 100 feet (30.5m).

The burial customs employed in these mounds varied. Some people's bodies were placed, along with elaborate grave goods, in coffinlike wooden containers, which were covered with earth. Other deceased individuals, perhaps of higher social rank, were interred in "charnel houses." These were hutlike structures made of wood and wattle. After performing various rituals, the mourners set them ablaze and then buried the remains beneath an earthen mound.

The Temple Mound Builders

Although archaeologists date the end of Hopewell culture and the beginning of the next mound-building civilization to circa A.D. 700, the transition was probably not abrupt. It is possible that large-scale crop failures, intertribal wars, or some other disasters contributed to the Hopewell decline. But the main reason for the rise of the next culture—which experts call the Mississippian—was likely fairly rapid adoption of new agricultural, social, and religious customs. In this way, Mississippian culture probably evolved from, rather than pushed aside and replaced, Hopewell culture.

A number of distinctive characteristics defined Mississippian culture, which dominated the Southeast for some eight hundred years or so. First, its people practiced intensive farming, particularly of corn, but also of beans, various gourds, and tobacco. (Tobacco was smoked, sniffed, or chewed in various religious ceremonies and also burned like incense or crushed and sprinkled in graves.) People still hunted and fished, but mainly as a supplement to agriculture.

The Mississippians also displayed a trend toward more centralized government and control of large expanses of territory. This new political system had powerful chiefs and a more complex

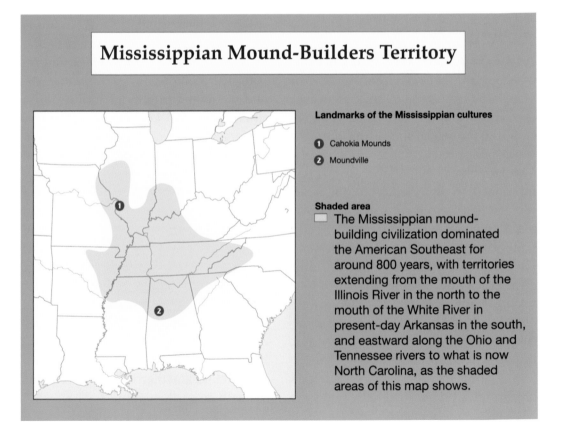

Mississippian Mound-Builders Territory

Landmarks of the Mississippian cultures

1. Cahokia Mounds
2. Moundville

Shaded area
☐ The Mississippian mound-building civilization dominated the American Southeast for around 800 years, with territories extending from the mouth of the Illinois River in the north to the mouth of the White River in present-day Arkansas in the south, and eastward along the Ohio and Tennessee rivers to what is now North Carolina, as the shaded areas of this map shows.

Cultural Contacts with Central America?

A number of archaeologists and other experts have pointed out certain similarities between the larger earthworks of the Mound Builders, especially those of the Mississippian phase, and the pyramids erected by the Maya, Aztec, and other Mesoamerican Indians. The latter, inhabiting what are now southern Mexico and some Central American countries, also had kings reminiscent of the great chiefs of the Mound Builders. So far, no firm evidence of any kind has been found showing that Mesoamericans migrated to or visited the southeastern United States. However, some researchers have suggested an alternate scenario. Perhaps, they say, on a few occasions individuals from the Mound Builder cultures traveled to Mesoamerica and saw the cities and pyramids there. Returning home, they may have incorporated some of the architectural ideas they had witnessed into their own large-scale works. Other scholars find this idea unlikely and suggest that the peoples of the two regions developed these ideas independently.

social structure with fairly rigid social classes. "These Indian groups," archaeologist Bruce D. Smith explains,

> attained a sophisticated chiefdom level of socio-political organization. Such chiefdoms are characterized by the existence of a family or kin grouping enjoying elite social and political status. At the top of the hierarchy [social-political ladder] was the chief, who, along with a small group of closely related kinsmen, made many of the important decisions that faced the society.[35]

As might be expected, the chiefs and other high-status individuals ate better foods and wore finer clothes than ordinary folk. The latter not only grew the food and made the clothes but also provided the labor needed to raise the mounds utilized by the elite class.

In fact, the manner in which Mississippian culture used its major mounds was another factor that set it apart from earlier mound-building societies. Some Mississippian mounds contained burials, like the Adena and Hopewell versions. But the Mississippians erected temples and houses atop their bigger mounds. For this reason, archaeologists sometimes call their society the Temple Mound Builder culture. The "temples" were lodges made of wood, wattle, and earth, in which chiefs and other community leaders conducted public rituals. These Indian nobles also lived in lavish quarters built on top of the larger mounds and were buried in these same mounds.

This model replicates the type of thatched hut made by the Cahokia.

The largest of the temple mounds, at Cahokia, in western Illinois, is 100 feet (30.5m) high and covers 16 acres (6.4ha). In its heyday, the Cahokia complex covered 3.8 square miles (10 sq. km) and supported a population of more than ten thousand. It seems to have been the capital of the most influential chiefdom in the Southeast, and its chief may have held sway over tens of thousands of miles of territory.

Decline of the Mound Builders

The Cahokia chiefdom and other Indian mini-nations of the Southeast were gone by the time white settlers arrived in the region. The reasons for the decline of Mound Builders are unknown, and numerous theories have been advanced to explain it. Most likely, a number of factors—perhaps overpopulation, climate change, crop failures, wars among chiefdoms, and so on—combined to break apart these peoples into the smaller tribal units that the first whites encountered.

These tribes often retained many of the Mound Builders' customs but practiced them on a smaller scale. An often-cited example is the Natchez tribe, which inhabited what is now southern Mississippi and whose ways were first documented by French explorers. "The Natchez had a central temple mound," Waldman points out, "and a nearby open plaza, as well as satellite mounds, some of them for houses and some for burials. The Natchez supreme ruler, the 'Great Sun,' lived on one of these." [36] Thus, like the pueblo-building Anasazi in the Southwest, the Mound Builders of the Southeast were another example of a great Indian civilization that reached its peak and then declined shortly before first contact with whites.

Chapter Six

Indians of the Northeastern Woodlands

The large Native American region most often called the Northeastern Woodlands stretched from the Atlantic coast westward to the Great Lakes. It included what are now the New England states (Maine, New Hampshire, Vermont, Massachusetts, Rhode Island, and Connecticut), the southern St. Lawrence River valley, Michigan, New York, Pennsylvania, New Jersey, coastal Virginia, and the northern Ohio River valley.

Almost all of this vast expanse, featuring several low mountain ranges and numerous lakes both large and small, was heavily forested and possessed abundant natural resources. The tribes that dwelled in the region took full advantage of these resources. Most hunted and foraged in the deep woods, some fished in the lakes and ocean estuaries, and some others supplemented these activities by raising corn and other crops.

A majority of the northeastern tribes belonged to two major branches—the Iroquoian speakers and the Algonquian speakers. Each was divided into many subgroups, with specific tribes or groups of tribes speaking dialects of one of these mother tongues. In New England, for instance, the Micmac (in Maine), Massachusett and Wampanoag (in Massachusetts), and Narragansett (in Rhode Island) were Algonquians. So were the Ottawa (in northern Michigan), Montauk (in Long Island), and Delaware (in Delaware). In contrast, Iroquoian dialects and customs prevailed among the Huron (in Ontario), Mohawk and Seneca (in New York), and Tuscarora (originally in southern Virginia).

Archaeologists presently believe that the Archaic Indian ancestors of both the Iroquois and Algonquians dwelled in the Northeast for many millennia. However, it appears that Algonquian groups predated the Iroquois in the regions of New York and New England. In the late first millennium A.D., or somewhat later, groups of Iroquois moved from an area farther south—perhaps Pennsylvania. They rapidly displaced a number of Algonquian tribes, especially in western and central New York, which became the principal Iroquois homeland.

Algonquian Lifeways

The establishment of the Iroquois in New York, and also in the area north of Lake Ontario, more or less divided the Algonquians into two geographically separate groups. The northern Algonquians, based in southern Canada, retained an Archaic lifestyle up to and beyond contact with white civilization. These peoples of the deep northern forests hunted, fished, and foraged but did not develop agriculture. Maintaining a seminomadic existence, they had no permanent villages. Instead, a typical band moved from month to month in a circuit within a given territory, seeking out moving animal herds and plants that bloomed seasonally. They heavily relied on birch bark, which they used to fashion storage

This illustration depicts an Algonquian village in 1585. It shows huts and longhouses inside a protective barricade.

Winning Over Tadodaho

One of the leading characters in the Iroquois story of the formation of their famous confederacy was an initial objector to the plan, the Onondagan war chief Tadodaho. Seneca scholar John C. Mohawk of the State University of New York at Buffalo provides these details about Tadodaho:

He was said to be the embodiment of evil, an individual who had woven snakes into his hair to intimidate all in his presence, and he had no interest in supporting a league dedicated to peace. The Peacemaker and Hiawatha despaired of ever converting him until they voiced their concerns to [a respected Iroquois woman named] Jikohnsaseh. She suggested that [Tadodaho] could be won over by being offered the chairmanship of the Great league. When the nations assembled to make their offer, Tadodaho accepted. Jikohnsaseh, who came to be described as the Mother of Nations or the Peace Queen, seized the horns of authority and placed them on Tadodaho's head in a gesture symbolic of the power of women in Iroquois [society].

John C. Mohawk, "Iroquois Confederacy," in Frederick E. Hoxie, *Encyclopedia of North American Indians.* Boston: Houghton Mifflin, 1996, p. 299.

containers, cooking utensils, and even canoes.

The so-called southern Algonquians, who inhabited New England, coastal New York and New Jersey, and Delaware, also hunted and fished. And those who lived near the ocean became adept at catching all manner of creatures that dwelled in estuaries and marshes (including various kinds of birds). As a result, they came to enjoy a phenomenally diverse and rich diet. At a single site once occupied by a group of Massachusett, archaeologists found the remains of food sources that included fox, mink, bear, beaver, deer, harbor seal, blue heron, mallard duck, hawk, eagle, snapping turtle, scallops, quahogs, snails, clams, sea bass, stingray, and many more.

Like other southern Algonquians (and *un*like the northern Algonquians), the Massachusett supplemented their hunting, fishing, and foraging with farming. They grew corn, squash, beans, and tobacco. The word *Massachusett* meant "people who live near the great hill." The exact location of said hill is unknown, for there were many low hills in the region they occupied—central and northern coastal Massachusetts (which of course is named for them).

The Massachusett spoke the same Algonquian dialect as their neighbors, the Wampanoag, Nauset, and Narragansett, indicating that all of these tribes were closely related. Indeed, these and many other Algonquian groups not only shared a language and the same ways of acquiring food, they also had similar ways of governing themselves. For example, each local group was organized as a type of political unit called a sachemship. It was overseen by a chieflike individual known as a sachem. Always a male, he made decisions for the group about land use, trade, and warfare; aiding him in these deliberations was a handful of men, often distinguished warriors, each of whom also enjoyed higher-than-normal social rank.

Southern Algonquians also shared similar religious ideas that revolved around a spirit world. It was inhabited by various supernatural beings and forces, including the souls of deceased ancestors, collectively called manitou. Each community had a shaman (a combination of priest and magician), called a *pawauog*, who communicated with the manitou, usually through dreams or waking visions. In this way, the spirits could offer advice and guidance to ordinary folk.

Another custom common to southern Algonquians, as well as northern ones, was erecting their characteristic dwelling—the wigwam. (This term was later used rather indiscriminately by white people to describe almost any Indian home, but technically it applied only to Algonquian houses.) According to one expert:

The wigwam could be easily constructed in less than a day. The typical wigwam was oval and consisted of saplings set in the ground and bent into arches and lashed [together with plant fibers]. The resultant frame was covered with large bark strips . . . leaving a smoke hole in the center and one end open for a doorway, which was covered with a hide or a woven rush [reed] mat.

An illustration depicts Metacomet, the sachem of the Wampanoags of New England. Algonquian tribes each had sachems, who made decisions for the group about land use, trade, and warfare.

A replica of an Algonquian wigwam is made from saplings and bark. Tribes that used it included the Massachusett, Nauset, and Narragansett.

. . . The finished structure could be up to 20 feet long and 14 feet wide, with walls 6 or 7 feet high and an overall height of 14 feet at the arch. The sleeping areas were arranged around the central fire and consisted of mats or cedar boughs and animal skins.[37]

Iroquois Lifeways

One advantage of the wigwam, especially for the more seminomadic Algonquians, was that it was easy and quick to put up or take down. In contrast, the most common dwellings of the Iroquois were larger, more elaborate, and more time-consuming to construct. They came to be called "longhouses" because even average-sized ones were 50 to 100 feet (15–30.5m) long; and some were exceptionally long—up to 300 feet (91.5m), the length of a football field.

A typical longhouse was shaped similarly to the Quonset huts built by the U.S. military during World War II, with a semicircular arched ceiling resting atop two vertical walls. The frame of the Iroquois version consisted of freshly cut young trees. The builders forced the bottoms of these saplings firmly into the ground and bent their tops over to form the curved ceiling. Then they covered this framework with thick layers of elm bark.

On the outside, the longhouses were arranged in fairly tight groups, likely partly for mutual protection. But further protection for the whole village was provided by a sturdy palisade (or stockade), a wooden perimeter wall made by lashing many small- and medium-sized tree trunks tightly together. (The fact that such walls existed shows that raids by Algonquian groups, or even other Iroquois groups, sometimes took place.)

These villages were semipermanent, but not because the Iroquois were nomadic. In fact, they were mainly farmers who stayed for many generations within fixed regions. However, they did periodically move around within these regions because of the manner in which they farmed—a technique now called "slash and burn." An Iroquois group or band first cleared an expanse of forest large enough to accommodate its village and fields. Then the people planted and harvested their crops for several seasons. But as happens in farmland everywhere, over time the soil became depleted of nutrients, severely reducing crop yields. Because they did not yet practice true crop rotation, after eight to ten years or so the Iroquois farmers had to move on. They cleared a swath of forest a few miles away and started over, which necessitated building a new village. "Relocation," Kopper points out, "also shifted the population away from plagues of fleas and to new sources of firewood, vital for winter warmth." [38]

This firewood was burned inside the longhouses, where the villagers slept

Longhouses are arranged in typical formation, in tight groups that were easy to defend.

year-round and cooked, ate, and socialized in the cold months. A hearth was situated about every 20 feet (6m) along a central aisle that ran down the middle of a longhouse. Usually two families shared each hearth, and members of these families slept on platforms raised somewhat from the floor on either side of the hearth.

The families living in a longhouse were related in that they were part of a larger kinship group—the clan. Unlike the clans of the Algonquians and most other North American Indians, the Iroquois versions were matrilineal, which meant that members traced their ancestry back through the female, rather than the male, line. A clause of an important Iroquois political document (originally preserved orally but later written down) states: "The lineal descent of the people . . . shall run in the female line. Women shall be considered the progenitors of the nation. They shall own the land and the soil. Men and women shall follow the status of the mother." [39]

Some of the customs that grew out of this female-oriented system affected marriage and the places where husbands and wives lived. A new groom, who had to be from a different clan than his bride's, left his own longhouse and moved into her longhouse, which was overseen by the oldest female in her clan.

An illustration depicts a medicine dance taking place inside a longhouse. These structures were semi-permanent and time-consuming to construct.

Iroquois Clans and Women

The New York State Museum provides this useful overview of the extended families and clans of the Iroquois and the important roles that women played in them:

Longhouses have another thing in common besides their shape. They were built to serve as a home for a large extended family. An extended family includes a number of family units consisting of parents and children, plus grandparents, aunts, uncles, cousins, etc. In an Iroquois longhouse there may have been 20 or more families which were all related through the mothers' side, along with the other relatives. All these families belonged to the same clan; each clan in a village had its own longhouse; the clans had branches in other villages. Clans were named for animals and birds; Turtle, Bear, and Hawk are examples. The symbol for the clan was used in decorations of household objects, in tattoos, and on the front of the longhouse. . . . The extended family not only shared the same building for their home, but they also worked together to make their living. The clan was the basic social and economic unit in Iroquois society and the leadership in the clans was through the women, because the kinship followed the mother's bloodline. The women managed the affairs of their longhouse, the farming, and distribution of food. They also selected the men who would represent their clan in the tribal council.

New York State Museum, "A Mohawk Iroquois Village." www.nysm.nysed.gov/IroquoisVillage/constructiontwo.html.

America's First Democracy?

This matrilineal system was strictly social in nature. In the political realm, the Iroquois chiefs who had charge of entire villages and tribes were male. Another aspect of Iroquois politics made it stand out from the politics of most other North American Indian groups. Namely, five of the major Iroquois tribes, all based in what is now New York State, came together in a major and long-lasting political alliance that the whites called the Iroquois Confederacy. The member tribes—the Mohawk, Oneida, Onondaga, Cayuga, and Seneca—called themselves the *Haudenosaunee*, roughly translated as "people of the longhouse." (In 1715, two centuries after the arrival of the whites, a sixth tribe, the Tuscarora, joined the Confederacy.)

The exact date and manner in which this famous Indian league formed remain uncertain. Some scholars think it emerged in the 1400s, shortly before contact with the whites. Others suspect the event occurred from one to three centuries earlier. As for

Wampum

Wampum, consisting of strands of decorative beads or shells, was used among the Iroquois and Algonquians to symbolize or conclude various important transactions or social or political events. This description of wampum comes from the constitution of the Iroquois Confederacy:

A bunch of shell strings is to be the symbol of the council fire of the Five Nations Confederacy. And the Lord whom the council of Fire Keepers shall appoint to speak for them in opening the council shall hold the strands of shells in his hands when speaking. When he finishes speaking he shall deposit the strings on an elevated place (or pole) so that all the assembled Lords and the people may see it and know that the council is open and in progress. When the council adjourns, the Lord who has been appointed by his comrade Lords to close it shall take the strands of shells in his hands and address the assembled Lords. Thus will the council adjourn until such time and place as appointed by the council. Then shall the shell strings be placed in a place for safekeeping.

Internet Modern History Sourcebook, "The Constitution of the Iroquois Confederacy." www.fordham. edu/halsall/mod/iroquois.html.

These bead necklaces would have been used as currency for trade between Native Americans and colonists of the region.

how the alliance came about, a founding story survived by word of mouth and was eventually written down. But it is impossible to know how much of it is accurate and how much is embellished or mere legend. The heroes of the story are a Huron, whom his fellow Iroquois called the Peacemaker, and his main supporter, a former Onondagan chief named Hiawatha. Supposedly, the Peacemaker asked the leaders of the five tribes to stop fighting one another and to live together in peace. In the words of one modern researcher:

> At each stop, he brought good fortune, and the people believed him. When he reached the Onandaga . . . he met Tadadaho, an evil man who would not consent to the union with the others. The Peacemaker persuaded him to relent by promising him that he could watch over the Council Fire. . . . When the representatives from the five nations reached the first league meeting, they had brought weapons. The Peacemaker had them bury their weapons beneath the Great Tree of Peace [and] then gave each an arrow. He broke an arrow to show that standing apart from each other, they are easily broken. He then bundled the arrows and failed to break them, showing the strength they will have if they stand together. [40]

In whatever manner the league formed, it proved to be highly success-ful. In large part this was because it was strong and bold enough to prevent wars among the tribes, but prudent and tactful enough to avoid intruding into the internal affairs of any one of them. "The confederacy was adaptive," Fagan says, "in that it allowed groups [of Iroquois] to legislate against unnecessary blood feuding, while still maintaining individual cultural and political identity in their dealings with others." [41]

The key to this flexibility was a thoughtful and effective constitution, or set of legal rules and procedures, which still survives. It calls for disputes to be decided by deliberation, discussion, and ultimately democratic voting among the member tribes. "First the question shall be [discussed and] passed upon by the Mohawk and Seneca Lords [league representatives]," one article says.

> Then it shall be discussed and passed by the Oneida and Cayuga Lords. Their decisions shall then be referred to the Onondaga Lords . . . for final judgment. . . . In all cases the procedure must be as follows. When the Mohawk and Seneca Lords have unanimously agreed upon a question, they shall report their decision to the Cayuga and Oneida Lords, who shall deliberate upon the question and report a unanimous decision to . . . the Onondaga, who shall render a decision as they see fit in case of a disagreement by the two bodies, or confirm the decisions of the two bodies if they are identical. [42]

Thus, in a sense the Onondaga acted like the U.S. vice president in his role as president of the Senate. He can break a tie vote among opposing groups of senators; similarly, the Onondagan representatives could end a standoff between the Mohawk-Seneca group and the Oneida-Cayuga group by siding with one or the other.

Some modern observers have noticed this and other similarities between the Iroquois constitution and the U.S. Constitution. And they suggest that the U.S. founders modeled their famous document partly on the older Indian one. However, this theory remains controversial and debated by scholars. What is more certain is that the first American political system that featured democratic ideals predated that of Thomas Jefferson, James Madison, and Alexander Hamilton by several centuries.

Chapter Seven

Indian Weapons and Intertribal Warfare

The precontact Native American groups and tribes of North America displayed an enormous variety of cultural differences, ranging from language to the ways they acquired food, erected their homes, and performed religious rituals. But one cultural factor that nearly all of these Indian groups shared was a natural tendency to fight one another. Indeed, intertribal warfare was common across the Americas long before the first whites arrived on the scene. Moreover, though individual weapons and tactics differed somewhat from place to place, most American Indians developed similar methods, styles, and rituals of fighting.

Reasons for Going to War

First, the motivations for fighting were similar among most Indians. For instance, grand political schemes, including large-scale conquest, acquiring big tracts of territory, and building up major military and political power, though common among Europeans, were very rare among Native Americans. Most Indians lacked well-defined national or state territories with recognized boundaries. Some tribes did inhabit certain regions for generations or even many centuries. But these areas were usually relatively small and often did not share boundaries with neighboring tribal areas.

Thus, acquiring territory was rarely a reason for fighting among Indians. More common motivations included such factors as intertribal rivalry or feuding, getting revenge for the killing of one's relatives or the seizure of captives. It was a custom among the Iroquois, for instance, to adopt such captives into the tribe to replace deceased members. In addition, some tribes looked on war as a sacred activity meant to restore the natural order of a given region, which the invisible spirits supposedly felt was somehow impaired or out of balance.

Mandans attack members of the Arikara in 1832. Intertribal warfare was a common feature of Native American society.

Sparked by such factors, precontact Indian wars were almost always local, small-scale, and lasted only a short period of time. This usually ensured that one's enemy would survive a conflict intact. "Instances of mass slaughter on the scale of those habitually carried out by the Assyrians, Greeks, Romans, Huns, Ottomans, and Spanish did not occur in aboriginal America," Cherokee historian Tom Holm points out. And as a result, intertribal conflicts almost never caused "the destruction of entire societies."[43]

Whatever the reasons for these conflicts, almost all precontact Native Americans shared some basic ideals related to warriors and fighting. A young man who went to war was expected to be brave, of course, but also honest and generous. In addition, he should display a high degree of training and especially discipline. "Indian discipline was founded on individual honor rather than corporal punishment," scholar Armstrong Starkey writes. And a sense of honor, along with some old-fashioned common sense, was expected of the commanders.

[War] leaders were chosen according to merit based on courage and experience [and] were concerned to save their men's lives and believed that victory did not justify unnecessary sacrifice. There was no disgrace in retreating to await a more favorable occasion for battle. . . . [Yet] while avoiding unnecessary casualties, the Indians were a martial people, ready to sell their lives dearly in defense of their homes.[44]

Probably not every warrior was able to live up to these ideals all of the time. However, strong social pressures and expectations made young Indian men strive to achieve them; and they experienced shame or even became social outcasts when they could not.

Offensive Weapons

No matter how brave a warrior was or how disciplined or well-trained he might be, he could not expect to be successful in battle without effective, reliable weapons. And creating such devices was always a challenge. Precontact Native American weapons were made entirely by hand and of largely unprocessed natural materials, including stone, wood, and in some cases unsmelted metals

(such as lumps of copper found in natural settings).

Offensive weapons (those used to attack an enemy) fell into three general groups—those for striking, those for cutting, and those for piercing. The oldest of the striking weapons were simple clubs fashioned of flint or jasper. Some examples had a rounded head, like that of a medieval European mace, while others had a head shaped like an ax blade. In another version, the head was not attached rigidly to the handle. Rather, it was placed inside a pouch of rawhide, which was attached to a wooden handle. Because the head stayed loose within the material, it imparted a small but damaging whiplash effect when the user swung the weapon. Still another kind of club

Fashioning Sharp Blade Edges

Indian knives with stone blades were highly effective weapons, mostly because the edges of the blades were extremely sharp. Weapons makers achieved this extraordinary sharpness by carefully chipping the relatively soft stone, a process called "flaking," described here by Colin F. Taylor, an expert on Native American weapons:

The natural edges or forms of the stone were modified by fracturing with a specially made flaking tool. The "flaker," as it was commonly called, had a blade generally of antler [deer or elk horn], ivory, or hard bone, set in a wooden handle. This was applied to the stone edge and, with a quick movement (at the same time exerting a strong pressure), a flake of the stone was forced off. A skilled individual worked rapidly, moving along the outline of the blade, producing a razor-sharp, although fragile, cutting edge.

Colin F. Taylor, *Native American Weapons*. Norman: University of Oklahoma Press, 2001, p. 37.

common to many North American Indians was made of wood or animal bone or both. Such clubs, which were used extensively in the Southwest and Northwest, could be used either in a traditional overhand stroke to crush a skull or arm, or in an upward stroke to shatter an opponent's jaw.

Cutting weapons wielded by precontact Native American warriors most often featured sharpened stone edges. The oldest and simplest version was a chisel-shaped blade made from a thin piece of jasper, flint, chert, or agate. When attached to a handle fashioned of wood, bone, or horn, the blade became a knife. (Another cutting weapon, the metal-bladed hatchet, required refined metals and industrial skills that precontact Indians did not possess; so it did not become common until after contact with white civilization.)

As for piercing weapons, the most common in the precontact period was for a long time the spear. It could be used in hand-to-hand combat, in which case the user jabbed it overhand at an opponent, not unlike the way ancient Greek soldiers jabbed their spears at their own enemies. More often however, the spear, or a shorter pointed shaft, was thrown, hurled, or propelled from a spot some distance from the target. Only rarely did Native Americans throw such spears or shafts using just the hand. Most often they used a second launching device, the earliest common example being the atlatl. Another device, used by the Miwok and Pomo in California, among others, consisted of a rawhide sling. And the Semi-noles, Choctaw, and Cherokee in the Southeast developed a blow tube; it worked by placing a short pointed shaft, or dart, in a hollow piece of sugarcane and forcefully blowing it out of the tube.

Still another propulsion system—the bow—made the arrow the most widely distributed American Indian piercing weapon after about A.D. 500–600. Virtually every tribe in North America eventually adopted the bow and arrow. The most prevalent kind of bow was the simple or self bow, made of a single piece of a bendable variety of wood, such as hickory, ash, or black locust. Another type of bow, the reinforced bow, was so named because the wood was backed by a strip of animal sinew to give it more flexibility and power. Reinforced bows were usually made of cedar, juniper, ash, or wild plum, though other kinds of wood were also used.

The arrows had heads fashioned from flint and other types of stone, as well as horn, bone, wood, seashell, and unprocessed copper. An arrowhead was most often triangular in shape. And the warrior joined it to the shaft by inserting it in a notch in the wood and lashing it tight with strips of sinew. It was also important that the shafts be straight and fitted with feathers to ensure balanced, accurate flight after leaving the bow. "A crooked arrow or one with improperly placed guide feathers proved worthless," Carlson points out. With great care, he says, the arrow makers

cut the shafts to the desired length and shape, tied them in a bunch,

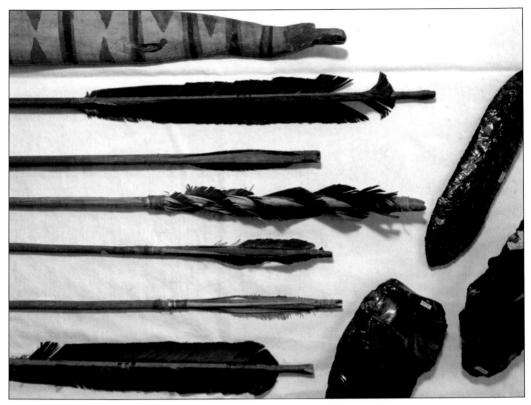

Arrows and stone cutting tools are displayed. The arrow at the center was used to kill a man from an enemy tribe.

and to season them hung them near a fire for about ten days. Then, in a tedious process [they] straightened the shafts. Over a period of several days, they used their teeth, grease, fire, and a special arrow straightener—a bone or horn with a hole slightly larger than the shaft through which they passed the arrow back and forth—to make the arrow perfectly round. . . . Next, they polished and painted the shaft. Finally, they attached the feathers—owl, turkey, or buzzard feathers preferred—with glue and fixed the point.[45]

Defensive Weapons and Measures

Precontact American Indians also employed various defensive military devices and methods. Many used body armor, although it was composed of wood, bone, ivory, and animal hides instead of processed metals, as much European armor was. An excellent example of wooden Indian armor is a surviving cuirass (chest protector) of the Tlingit people, who dwelled in the Northwest Coast region. The front section contains ten vertical wooden slats bound together with strips of animal sinew and rawhide. Attached to the end slats are sections made of lightweight, somewhat flexible wooden rods, also placed vertically. Wide rawhide strips attached to the top of the front section of the armor ran back over the wearer's shoulders and connected to the back section, which was made of slats like the front. The Huron and some other Iroquois groups of the Northeast also wore elaborate armor composed of wooden rods and slats. (A European drawing made shortly before 1660 shows a Huron warrior wearing such an outfit.)

In addition, the Tlingit and some other Indian groups used protective helmets.

They made these from either bundles of small wooden rods or a single, carved piece of wood. Some Tlingit helmets even had movable visors similar to those on the metal helmets of medieval European knights.

Another common kind of Native American armor was crafted from layers of animal hides. Some northwestern tribes used it, as did the Shoshone, Pawnee, and several other plains tribes, the Navajo in the Southwest, and the Mohawk in New York. Such armor usually featured two or more layers of hide stitched together with rawhide strips. Elk hide was widely used, although hides from moose, buffalo, and other large mammals were also employed in various areas. Hide armor was also used to protect the horses of the Shoshone and some other plains peoples.

Another kind of defensive device used widely by American Indians was a circular (or occasionally rectangular) shield made of tree bark, wood, dried animal hides, or sometimes a combination of these materials. The Comanche, in the southern plains, carried a version fashioned from two pieces of rawhide laced together around a wooden hoop. The space in the middle was stuffed with feathers, grass, horse hair, or some other pliable, or bendable, material to help slow the momentum of a club or arrow. Most such shields were about three feet (1m) in

An Indian warrior is shown with a protective shield and a spear. Before contact with whites, shields would have been made out of wood and/or dried animal hides.

Whites Adopt Indian Armor

Although on occasion some American Indian tribes did copy various elements of the armor they saw worn by early white explorers, the process often worked the other way around. That is, a number of early white settlers who lacked armor adopted already existing native versions. A memorable example is the case of Captain John Smith, the renowned cofounder of the English colony of Jamestown, in Virginia. In 1608 he found himself under attack by a local tribe. A different tribe, which had established friendship with Smith and the other whites, helped him and his men put on Indian-made wooden armor. This armor was so effective that, in the words of one of the white participants, it "securely beat back the savages from off the plain without [our receiving] any hurt."

Quoted in Colin F. Taylor, *Native American Weapons*. Norman: University of Oklahoma Press, 2001, p. 123.

diameter and featured a neck strap that allowed a warrior to carry his shield on his side, shoulder, or back. Many Indians felt that their shields could be made to possess supernatural properties that increased the owners' level of protection. To that end, they painted on the shields designs meant to invoke the powers of various spirits or animal or sky gods.

A certain amount of military protection was also gained by various kinds of defense structures used by precontact Indians, particularly those who lived in the Southwest and Eastern Woodlands. Some of these defenses were quite large and elaborate, notably the wooden stockades erected by the Iroquois around their villages. Sometimes earthen embankments (or raised areas of dirt) were built outside the stockade for extra protection. Some northeastern Indians also created moatlike ditches to help keep attackers from entering the village.

In the Southwest, in contrast, fortifications seem to have been designed more to protect a central ceremonial center and/or members of an elite social class. "Many of the principal towns erected by the southeastern tribes were religious sanctuaries as well as . . . administrative centers," scholar Norman Bancroft-Hunt explains.

The descriptions we have suggest these towns were protected by palisades [fences], ditches, and earth embankments, and sometimes even by moats, with the house of the chief, the temples of the priests, and the dwellings of other dignitaries raised on earthen mounds protected by secondary palisades or walls. By far the

Intimidation as a Battle Tactic

With rare exceptions, large-scale armies divided into distinct formations and executing formal battlefield tactics, a tactic widely used in Europe, was unknown in native North America. Among those exceptions were the tactics used by some Florida tribes, including the Calusa, Timucua, and Apalachee, who fielded hundreds of warriors at one time. It is questionable, however, how many of the troops in these armies actually participated in combat. Amassing such a large army appears to have been intended mainly for show, probably to intimidate or frighten the enemy. According to French explorers who witnessed such battles, only a minority of the warriors actually fought one another. Instead, as the two armies faced each other across an open field, groups of warriors from one army shouted insults at their opponents. They also stepped forward, brandished [waved] their weapons, and screamed high-pitched war cries. Members of the enemy army then did the same. Meanwhile, small bands of selected warriors from each army would slip away, hopefully unnoticed, and attack small groups of troops on the fringes of the enemy army. After a few hours of such minor skirmishing, which resulted in few deaths, the armies retired and the battle was over.

Native American warriors often branched off from larger groups and engaged the enemy in small skirmishes.

larger part of the population lived outside these massive fortifications, and the only permanent occupancy was by an exclusive class of civil, military, and religious leaders, who were guarded by warrior societies whose specific function was to protect the nobility and priests.[46]

War Tactics and Rituals

Thus, Indians living all across North America developed similar (though not necessarily identical) modes of military offense and defense. The actual strategies and tactics they used fell into four broad forms or categories, with numerous minor variations from place to place. In the open plains and other nonforested areas, it was common for opposing warriors to line up opposite each other and fire atlatls or arrows back and forth. Because shields were used by both sides, casualties were usually very light; and after a while the opposing forces would go home, feeling satisfied that they had vented their anger.

A second, more lethal kind of combat involved a war chief leading his men in a charge that led to hand-to-hand combat with clubs or knives. The outcome was generally brief and bloody. The third general kind of combat, consisting of what are now called guerrilla tactics, was common in both the Eastern Woodlands and the mountainous areas of the Southwest. The warriors usually spread out and took advantage of trees, rocks, and other forms of cover. The fourth major tactical approach, one practiced all across

the continent, was to launch raids on enemy villages or camps. Such raids most often took place before dawn so that the attackers could take advantage of the darkness and the fact that most of the enemy were sleeping. Typically, the raiders swept into the village, killed a number of victims swiftly, and then slipped away before the survivors could organize a proper defense.

The warriors who achieved a successful raid or other military victory acquired much prestige in their community. But sometimes such attacks failed. This was a problem for the attackers because their people might view them as cowards or pathetic losers. To avoid such an outcome, many Indian groups developed special war rituals that substituted for actual combat. When Tlingit raiders were unable to penetrate an enemy village, for example, they put on a loud, spirited display of intimidation instead. The warriors climbed into canoes, rowed to a point within shouting distance of the village, verbally taunted the villagers, and called on various gods and spirits to curse them. To save face, the villagers then produced their own shaman, who aimed a similar barrage of curses and threats at the raiders. Finally, the intruders departed, leaving behind few or no casualties on either side.

Similar mock battle rituals developed among numerous other American tribes. This was one of the reasons that their wars, unlike so many fought in Europe and the Middle East in the same period, rarely, if ever, wiped out entire towns or peoples.

Epilogue

The Coming of
the Whites

After Columbus initiated European contact with the native peoples of the Americas, the Spanish and the Portuguese were quick to begin colonizing and exploiting the new lands. The English, French, Dutch, and others soon followed suit. And so began the final chapter in the long saga of the North American Indians. Unfortunately for them, it was to be, in Fagan's words, "five centuries of catastrophic and disruptive cultural change in the face of an inexorable [relentless] European presence." [47] In short, the white onslaught—consisting of naked theft of Indian lands, infection of the natives with deadly diseases, massacres of those who resisted, and the forcible herding of the survivors onto remote reservations—decimated traditional Native American civilization.

Outnumbered and Outarmed

The manner in which whites invaded and rapidly disrupted American Indian cultures with lethal results is well illustrated by the sad fate of the Massachusett tribe. Some of the earliest white explorers to reach southern New England brought germs with them. Most of the whites had immunity or at least a high level of resistance to the diseases these germs caused. But the local Indians did not. As a result, between 1614 and 1617, epidemics wiped out three-quarters of the Massachusett, many of whom had never even seen a white person. This is why, when the Pilgrims landed at Plymouth in 1620, most of the native villages in the area were already abandoned. And when the Puritans began settling farther north, at Boston, nine years later, only about five hundred Massachusett were left alive. By 1640 that tribe had, for all intents and purposes, ceased to exist. Most of the scattered remaining members were killed by whites in wars in the following few decades. Only a tiny handful of Massachusett survived, their pitiable fate to live in poverty and squalor on the edges of white communities.

This same scenario, or one very similar to it, was repeated again and again in every region of the United States. One motivation for these conquests was that most whites looked on Indians as inferiors, both racially and spiritually. Particularly strong among whites was the religious attitude that the natives must either convert to Christianity or pay the consequences. "Frustration over Indian 'wickedness' in refusing to accept either Christ or 'civilization,'" Kopper writes, led many whites "to condemn the natives as hopeless, vicious, and undeserving."[48]

The whites had more than a superior attitude. They also possessed a strong arsenal of logistical and other advantages that the Indians were ultimately unable to counter. In addition to the debilitating diseases the whites brought with them, they had advanced weapons, including guns and cannons. The whites also had superior numbers. By 1820 the United States had a population of roughly 10 million, compared to fewer than half a million Indians living in and west of the Ohio River valley. And over time, the U.S. Army grew steadily bigger and better organized. More soldiers, more horses, and more guns, plus expanding networks of railroads and advanced communications, including the telegraph, all worked against the Indians, who were increasingly on the defensive. "Neither stealthy ambushes nor full-scale assaults [by Indians] could stem the unending stream of white reinforcements," says scholar Peter Nabokov. "In the end, the Indian was simply outnumbered as well as outarmed. Warfare against the whites was at best only a holding action. Native fighting prowess was judged finally by how long a tribe could prolong its retreat or delay its surrender."[49]

Trails of Tears

Even when various tribes had given up fighting the white intruders, the latter were usually not satisfied with merely defeating and humiliating the Indians. Believing Native Americans to be inferior and potentially dangerous, many whites did not want them to live among or even near them. So the U.S. government adopted a particularly inhumane new policy. It consisted of removing Indians from their ancestral lands and relocating them in remote, unfamiliar, less productive ones.

The relocation of numerous southeastern tribes in the 1830s remains among the most vivid, terrifying, and heartrending examples of this policy. Though nearly all of the tribes in the region had been defeated or neutralized by the late 1820s, tens of thousands of Cherokee, Creek, Choctaw, and others still lived there. Viewing this situation as intolerable, in 1830 Congress passed the Indian Removal Act. With cold, unsympathetic efficiency, white soldiers proceeded to move entire villages and peoples west of the Mississippi to a special region that whites had designated "Indian Country." (It consisted of parts of what are now Oklahoma, Kansas, and Nebraska.)

Some of these Indians courageously resisted. Perhaps the most famous case

An illustration depicts the mass deaths that occurred among Native Americans with the coming of smallpox.

was that of the Cherokee, who lived in Georgia. When they refused to move, President Martin Van Buren sent some seven thousand troops against them. The soldiers dragged the Cherokee from their houses and drove them in a forced march westward, an ordeal that became known as the "Trail of Tears." Each day, dozens of Cherokee died of starvation, exposure to freezing temperatures, or sickness. "The sick and the feeble were carried in wagons," a white witness later recalled.

Even aged females, apparently nearly ready to drop into the grave, were traveling with heavy burdens attached to the back—on the sometimes frozen ground, and sometimes muddy streets, with no covering for the feet except what nature had given them. . . . They buried fourteen or fifteen [Cherokee] at every stopping place.[50]

In all, more than four thousand Cherokee died before the tribe reached its destination in Indian Country in 1839. Meanwhile, back in Georgia, gangs of whites looted the empty Cherokee houses and burned them to the ground.

The Edge of Extinction

Despite the many defeats of and atrocities perpetrated against the eastern Indians up to that time, most western Indians did not see their own demise as inevitable. If they were brave enough, they reasoned, and if they fought hard enough and summoned the powers of their gods and spirits, maybe they could stop the white advance. This attitude was common among the Sioux, Cheyenne, Arapaho, and other plains tribes. Their warriors raided white outposts and wagon trains, hoping to stop whites from seizing their hunting grounds. In retaliation, the U.S. Army launched campaign after devastating campaign against them.

The climax of these so-called "Indian Wars" took place in late December 1890. U.S. cavalry units surrounded a small group of Sioux, including many women and children, along Wounded Knee Creek in South Dakota. When the soldiers tried to arrest the Indians, someone—whether a soldier or an Indian is unknown—fired a weapon, which touched off a massacre. The white troops fired repeatedly at the unarmed natives, killing 153 of them.

After that, there was no more native resistance against the whites. Most surviving Indians now lived in poverty on reservations, their movements restricted,

The massacre at Wounded Knee occurred when government troops attacked a mostly unarmed group of Sioux on December 20, 1890.

their civil rights severely limited, and their futures bleak. The results of the great migrations that had peopled the continent over the course of many millennia had been in a sense erased and negated by speedier, more forceful white migrations. In this way, North America came to be peopled twice, once slowly and peacefully and once rapidly and violently. In the same year as the Wounded Knee massacre, the Sioux chief Black Elk summed up the plight of a formerly populous, diverse, and culturally rich group of peoples now tottering on the edge of extinction: "Once we were happy in our own country and we were seldom hungry. . . . But the Wasichus [whites] came, and they have made little islands for us . . . and always these islands are becoming smaller, for around them surges the gnawing flood of the Wasichus."[51]

Notes

Introduction: Challenges to Learning About the Past

1. Edmund J. Ladd, "Archaeology and Indians," in Frederick E. Hoxie, *Encyclopedia of North American Indians*. Boston: Houghton Mifflin, 1996, p. 33.
2. Quoted in Ladd, "Archaeology and Indians," p. 34.
3. Brian M. Fagan, *Ancient North America*. New York: Thames and Hudson, 2005, p. 67.
4. Fagan, *Ancient North America,* p. 68.

Chapter One: Origins of the American Indians

5. *Internet Medieval Sourcebook*, "Extracts from the Journal of Christopher Columbus." www.fordham.edu/halsall/source/columbus1.html.
6. *Indigenous Peoples' Literature*, "Chelan Creation Myth: Creation of the First Indians," Indians.org. www.indians.org/welker/firstind.htm.
7. See 2 Kings 17:6.
8. Quoted in PBS, *NOVA*, "Where Are the Ten Lost Tribes?" www.pbs.org/wgbh/nova/israel/losttribes2.html.
9. Quoted in E. James Dixon, *Quest for the Origins of the First Americans*. Albuquerque: University of New Mexico Press, 1993, p. 3.
10. Quoted in Brian M. Fagan, *The Great Journey: The Peopling of Ancient America*. Miami: University Press of Florida, 2003, p. 34.

11. Philip Kopper, *The Smithsonian Book of North American Indians*. New York: Harry N. Abrams, 1986, p. 31.
12. Fagan, *Great Journey*, pp. 133–34.

Chapter Two: The Peopling of North America

13. Fagan, *Ancient North America*, p. 91.
14. Fagan, *Ancient North America*, p. 89.
15. Quoted in Kopper, *Smithsonian Book of North American Indians*, p. 40.
16. Quoted in *Space Daily*, "New Clovis-Age Comet Impact Theory," May 23, 2007. www.spacedaily.com/reports/New_Clovis_Age_Comet_Impact_Theory_999.html.
17. Arrell M. Gibson, *The American Indian: Prehistory to the Present*. Lexington, MA: D.C. Heath, 1980, p. 21.

Chapter Three: Indians of the American West

18. Quoted in Kopper, *Smithsonian Book of North American Indians*, p. 201.
19. Kopper, *Smithsonian Book of North American Indians*, p. 217.
20. Kopper, *Smithsonian Book of North American Indians*, p. 191.
21. Quoted in Kopper, *Smithsonian Book of North American Indians*, p. 193.
22. Carl Waldman, *Atlas of the North American Indian*. New York: Facts On File, 1985, p. 39.
23. Waldman, *Atlas of the North American Indian*, p. 18.
24. Gibson, *The American Indian*, p. 75.

Chapter Four: Native Tribes of the Great Plains

25. Waldman, *Atlas of the North American Indian,* pp. 39–40.
26. Fagan, *Ancient North America,* pp. 131–32.
27. Fagan, *Ancient North America,* p. 134.
28. Quoted in Frederick E. Hoxie, ed., *Encyclopedia of North American Indians.* Boston: Houghton Mifflin, 1996, p. 224.
29. Quoted in Fagan, *Ancient North America,* p. 138.
30. Paul H. Carlson, *The Plains Indians.* College Station: Texas A&M University Press, 1998, p. 39.
31. Gibson, *The American Indian,* pp. 244–45.

Chapter Five: Early Inhabitants of the Southeast

32. Thomas Jefferson, *Notes on the State of Virginia,* chap. 11, American Studies at the University of Virginia. http://xroads.virginia.edu/~hyper/JEFFERSON/ch11.html.
33. James A. Brown, "Mound Builders," in Hoxie, *Encyclopedia of North American Indians,* p. 398.
34. Fagan, *Ancient North America,* p. 418.
35. Quoted in Kopper, *Smithsonian Book of North American Indians,* pp. 164–65.
36. Waldman, *Atlas of the North American Indian,* p. 22.

Chapter Six: Indians of the Northeastern Woodlands

37. Quoted in Hoxie, *Encyclopedia of North American Indians,* pp. 680–81.
38. Kopper, *Smithsonian Book of North American Indians,* p. 140.

39. *Internet Modern History Sourcebook,* "The Constitution of the Iroquois Confederacy." www.fordham.edu/halsall/mod/iroquois.html.
40. Brian Cook, "The Iroquois Confederacy." www.campton.sau48.k12.nh.us/iroqconf.htm.
41. Fagan, *Ancient North America,* p. 505.
42. *Internet Modern History Sourcebook,* "The Constitution of the Iroquois Confederacy."

Chapter Seven: Indian Weapons and Intertribal Warfare

43. Tom Holm, "Warriors and Warfare," in Hoxie, *Encyclopedia of North American Indians,* p. 666.
44. Armstrong Starkey, *European and Native American Warfare, 1675–1815.* Norman: University of Oklahoma Press, 1998, pp. 21–22.
45. Carlson, *The Plains Indians,* p. 62.
46. Norman Bancroft-Hunt, *Warriors: Warfare and the Native American Indian.* London: Salamander, 1995, pp. 22–23.

Epilogue: The Coming of the Whites

47. Fagan, *Ancient North America,* p. 511.
48. Kopper, *Smithsonian Book of North American Indians,* p. 277.
49. Peter Nabokov, ed., *Native American Testimony.* New York: Harper and Row, 1978, p. 95.
50. Quoted in John Ehle, *Trail of Tears: The Rise and Fall of the Cherokee Nation.* New York: Doubleday, 1988, pp. 357–58.
51. Quoted in Gibson, *The American Indian,* p. 426.

For Further Reading

Books

Paul H. Carlson, *The Plains Indians*. College Station: Texas A&M University Press, 1998. An excellent overview of the history and customs of the Horse and Bison culture of the plains.

E. James Dixon, *Quest for the Origins of the First Americans*. Albuquerque: University of New Mexico Press, 1993. Examines the earliest North American cultures and how they flourished.

Brian M. Fagan, *Ancient North America*. New York: Thames and Hudson, 2005. This is an excellent, highly detailed study of precontact North American Indians, broken down by geographic region.

———, *The Great Journey: The Peopling of Ancient America*. Miami: University Press of Florida, 2003. A compelling exploration of the current theories for when and how the first Native Americans arrived in North America.

Arrell M. Gibson, *The American Indian: Prehistory to the Present*. Lexington, MA: D.C. Heath, 1980. An information-packed overview of Native American peoples, with a useful section on their earliest settlements.

Philip Kopper, *The Smithsonian Book of North American Indians*. New York: Harry N. Abrams, 1986. Examines the early Native American cultures by region. Beautifully illustrated.

Allison Lassieur, *Before the Storm: American Indians Before the Europeans*. New York: Facts On File, 1998. Aimed at high school–level readers, this well-organized book examines early Indian cultures in various regions of North America.

George R. Milner, *The Moundbuilders: Ancient Peoples of Eastern North America*. New York: Thames and Hudson, 2005. A fascinating study of the early Native Americans who erected the mysterious mounds in the Ohio Valley and elsewhere.

Paul E. Minnis, *People and Plants in Ancient Western North America*. New York: HarperCollins, 2004. Explores the earliest Native American cultures on the continent and how they utilized existing plants and other resources.

Heather Pringle, *In Search of Ancient North America: An Archaeological Journey to Forgotten Cultures*. New York: Wiley, 1996. Tells how archaeologists have worked diligently to unearth evidence of the early peopling of the continent.

Colin F. Taylor, *Native American Weapons*. Norman: University of Oklahoma Press, 2001. The most comprehensive available study of Indian weapons, both offensive and defensive.

Web Sites

America's Stone Age Explorers (www. pbs.org/wgbh/nova/stoneage). A site related to the *NOVA* series on early Americans, with several links to related articles.

Ancestors of the New World Had Many Origins (www.cabrillo.edu/~crsmith/ ancestorsmanyorigins.html). Some anthropological evidence suggests that the earliest immigrants to North America came from Japan and China.

The Bering Land Bridge (www.cabrillo. edu/~crsmith/bering.html). Good overview of the discovery of the Bering land bridge and its role in allowing ancient migrations from Asia into North America.

Clovis People (www.crystalinks.com/ clovis.html). A brief but informational overview of the so-called Clovis Culture and its artifacts.

History of American Archaeology (www. mnsu.edu/emuseum/archaeology/arc haeology/timeline/history2.html). An excellent synopsis of North American archaeological efforts, presented in a convenient chronological breakdown.

Kennewick Man (www.mnh.si.edu/ arctic/html/kennewick_man.html). A useful overview of the discovery of this early North American hunter, by James C. Chatters, one of the first scientists to study the remains.

The Woodland Period (www.nps.gov/ history/seac/woodland.htm). An overview of the history and customs of the Eastern Woodlands Indian groups.

Index

Picture Credits

Cover photo: © George H.H. Huey / Corbis

AP Images, 11, 85

The Art Archive / Chateau du Grand-Pressigny / Gianni Dagli Orti / The Picture Desk, Inc., 27

The Art Archive / Gianni Dagli Orti / The Picture Desk, Inc., 6, 7 (top left)

The Art Archive / Gift of William Weiss / Buffalo Bill Historical Center, Wyoming / 23.62 / The Picture Desk, Inc., 55

The Art Archive / Gift of W. J. (Bill) Holcombe, Bear Creek Ranch, Dubois, Wyoming, Buffalo Bill Historical Center, Cody, Wyoming / 14.98 / The Picture Desk, Inc., 31

The Art Archive / Monastery of the Rabida, Palos, Spain / Gianni Dagli Orti / The Picture Desk, Inc., 7 (top right)

The Art Archive / Musee du Nouveau Monde La Rochelle, Gianni Dagli Orti / The Picture Desk, Inc., 49

© Bettmann / Corbis, 93

Bildarchiv Preussischer Kulturbesitz / Art Resource, NY, 41

© British Museum / Art Resource, NY, 71

© Christie's Images / Corbis, 88

© Richard A. Cooke / Corbis, 63, 68

© Corbis, 40, 53

Photograph by Edward S. Curtis. The Library of Congress, 7 (bottom)

© Franz-Marc Frei / Corbis, 9

© Gianni Dagli Orti / Corbis, 30

© Mark E. Gibson / Corbis, 37

© George H. H. Huey / Corbis, 47

© Glyn Jones / Corbis, 86

© Mary Evans Picture Library / The Image Works, 73

© Warren Morgan / Corbis, 25

MPI / Getty Images, 78

Copyright © North Wind / North Wind Picture Archives—All rights reserved, 14, 19, 20, 29, 36, 43, 45, 50, 60, 75, 76, 92

Reproduced by permission of Gale, a part of Cengage Learning, 10, 44, 57, 66

© Anders Ryman / Corbis, 17

Smithsonian American Art Museum, Washington, DC / Art Resource, NY, 52, 82

© Marilyn Angel Wynn / Nativestock Pictures / Corbis, 38, 74

About the Author

Historian and award-winning author Don Nardo has written many books for young people about American history, including *The Salem Witch Trials*; *The American Revolution*; *The Mexican-American War*; *The Declaration of Independence*; several volumes on the history and culture of Native Americans, and biographies of presidents Thomas Jefferson, Andrew Johnson, and Franklin D. Roosevelt. Nardo lives with his wife, Christine, in Massachusetts.